Victorian High Society

Victorian High Society

STELLA MARGETSON

B. T. BATSFORD LTD • LONDON

With love to darling Judith

BY THE SAME AUTHOR

Journey by Stages

Leisure and Pleasure in the Nineteenth Century

Leisure and Pleasure in the Eighteenth Century

Fifty Years of Victorian London

Regency London

The Long Party

First published 1980
ISBN 0 7134 1218 6
Set in Goudy by Modern Text Typesetting
Southend-on-Sea, Essex
Printed in England by Butler & Tanner Ltd
Frome, Somerset
for the publishers B T Batsford Ltd
4 Fitzhardinge Street London W1H 0AH

CONTENTS

LIST OF ILLUSTRATIONS

Unacknowledged photographs are from the author's collection.

ACKNOWLEDGMENT

The nineteenth century is so rich in contemporary diaries, letters and memoirs, to say nothing of periodicals such as the *Illustrated London News* and *Punch*, that to enumerate all my sources of material would be an impossible task. But I would like to acknowledge the great debt I owe to the authors, editors and publishers of the works listed in the Bibliography at the end of this book and to thank them for helping me to understand the Victorians in high Society.

INTRODUCTION

Nothing now seems more remote than the world of Victorian high Society with its elaborate ritual of country house parties and the London Season, its pride and exclusiveness and its almost unbelievable opulence. But the Victorians themselves took the rigid class structure of nineteenth-century England for granted and to them it did not appear in the least strange that the nobility and gentry of 'the great world' as Thackeray called it, should live in splendid style.

The importance attached to birth and breeding was no accident. It endowed the leading aristocratic families with great power and privilege. They were born to rule and lead; they guided the destiny of the nation. They owned the land, the green pastures, the parks and pleasure grounds they had inherited from their ancestors, and they employed a vast number of people on their estates without abusing the loyal service they received. For the English upper classes, unlike their continental neighbours in France and Germany, had a strong sense of duty towards those less fortunate than themselves, and it was this that enabled them to survive and prosper and to earn the respect of the common people.

They also had a strong belief in their own superiority. They *were* Society: superior even to the rather dull and very proper Court of the young Queen Victoria and her Teutonic husband, Prince Albert of Saxe-Coburg and Gotha. They never liked Prince Albert. He was not a hunting man; he was an intellectual and a foreigner, and he played the organ. But after his death in 1861 and the withdrawal of the widowed Queen into a life of perpetual sorrow, her eldest son, the Prince of Wales, became the leader of fashionable Society and Marlborough House its centre of gaiety, pleasure and cosmopolitan brilliance.

By the 1870s birth and breeding no longer counted as the first element in Society; money became the means of entering the magic circle. Rich industrialists, bankers and East India merchants bought their way in by setting themselves up as landowners and country gentlemen. They went hunting, shooting and racing with His Royal Highness. They sent their sons to public schools and married their daughters to the not so rich, younger sons of the gentry, and if they behaved well, they were accepted with a good grace.

Clothes were spectacular and jewellery blazed on the ample bosoms of the ladies. Balls, dinner parties and receptions were grand and very formal, hedged about with etiquette and the unwritten laws of what could, or could not, be done in good Society. Carriages were spick and span, houses large and luxurious and servants plentiful. Successful architects, painters and writers made their way up the ladder and social climbers with feminine beauty or masculine *bonhomie* could sometimes gain an entrée into the most exclusive drawing-rooms.

But it is dangerous to generalize about the Victorians; they were so individual. This book with its contemporary illustrations is an attempt to show how the upper classes passed their time, what they believed in and how they behaved in the great world of high Society, which no longer exists and will never return.

F. SMYTH.

1
Society and the Court

In 1837 when Queen Victoria held her first Drawing-Room at St James's Palace, the distinguished company crowding the State Apartments came to appraise her. She had led such a restricted life under the eye of her quarrelsome and hot-tempered mother, the Duchess of Kent, no one knew what to expect of her. Had she inherited the dreadful tantrums and self-indulgence of her late uncle, King George IV, or the undignified, vulgar behaviour of his brother, King William IV? Would the vicious character of the Duke of Cumberland and the bumbling stupidity of the Duke of Sussex be found in her nature? Or, as Lord Melbourne's sister, Lady Cowper rather gushingly suggested, was she really 'as great a wonder as Fair Star or any other Princess with the good fortune to be peculiarly gifted by the Fairies with *le Don de Plaisir*'?

Elderly gentlemen of the aristocratic Whig and Tory families who governed the country and filled the high offices of state, were moved to tears by the palpable sincerity of the young Queen. Their haughty ladies, quizzing her with a far more critical eye, on the whole were satisfied with what they saw. She was not a beauty. She was rather dumpy, plump and pink-cheeked, with prominent blue eyes and small teeth protruding over her lower lip. But in contrast to those wicked uncles of hers, with their brandy-coloured faces and swollen legs, who had so debauched the Royal House of Hanover, there was a charming, youthful freshness about her and for anyone so young, she had a quite extraordinary natural dignity.

She was high-spirited, too, and full of vitality. She loved dancing and riding, singing and playing at battledore and shuttlecock, these girlish diversions in no way intruding upon her seriousness of purpose or her remarkable capacity for attending to the business of the monarchy. Far from being frightened of those bulky red leather boxes stuffed to the brim with state papers, she revelled in them and was quick to learn. 'I get so many papers to sign every day that I have a *very great* deal to do,' she wrote in her Journal, adding, 'I *delight* in the work', and again, 'I receive so many communications from my ministers, but I like it very much.'

She liked even more the feeling of independence she now enjoyed. It was not surprising if it went to her head a little and that when she moved into

1 The distinguished company attending the Drawing-Room held by Queen Victoria at St James's Palace: the ladies *en grande-toilette*, the gentlemen in full court dress

Buckingham Palace, her own apartments were at the farthest distance possible from those she allotted to her mother. For the first time she was mistress of her own household, not just a counter pushed this way and that in the sticky game of the royal succession. For the first time Society paid homage to her, and surrounded by the Yeomen of the Guard in scarlet and gold, the Gentlemen of the Household in full court dress and members of the *Corps Diplomatique* in their fancy uniforms, she was the absolute centre of attraction at her Drawing-Room as the débutantes, in their feather plumes and off-the-shoulder gowns with narrow waists and flowing skirts of tulle, curtsied to kiss her hand before withdrawing backwards out of her royal presence. It was all very exciting, very colourful and very stimulating. Her Maids of Honour admired her jewellery, the diadem shining in her light brown hair, the pearls and diamonds cascading over her small bosom, the Garter sash and star glittering on her embroidered pink silk gown. And they admired her royal carriage, the way she held her head and the way she walked. There was no mistaking who she was, even when she laughed, as she often did, opening her mouth wide and showing her not very pretty pink gums, or when she knelt on the floor to bath her little dog Dash.

She was careful not to abuse her sovereignty, though it soon became evident that she knew her own mind and would not be thwarted – hence the bedchamber crisis in 1839, which shook the Court profoundly. The time had come when Lord Melbourne, her first Prime Minister, to whom she was utterly devoted, could not continue to govern with his small majority in the House of Commons and the Queen had to send for Sir Robert Peel, the leader of the Tory opposition. Compared with Melbourne, he was awkward, lacking in social grace and warmth and did not at that time recommend himself to the Queen at all. She took an instant dislike to him and was horrified when he suggested that a change in the Royal Household would be necessary, since her Ladies of the Bedchamber and Gentlemen in Waiting had all been appointed by Melbourne and were naturally his supporters. Indeed she was so angry with Sir Robert, she refused outright to give up any of her ladies and even the intervention of the Duke of Wellington had no effect on her obstinacy. 'The Queen of England will *not* submit to such trickery!' she told him, whereupon the warrior Duke had to admit to an inglorious defeat – there was nothing more to be said. Melbourne patched up his tottering Government and the Whig ladies continued to serve Her Majesty.

She had already incurred the displeasure of the Tories by her behaviour towards Lady Flora Hastings, a Lady-in-Waiting to the Duchess of Kent, who, it was whispered about the Court, had committed a misdemeanour with Sir John Conroy, a very dubious gentleman in attendance upon the Duchess. Lady Tavistock, Lady Portman and the Queen's all-powerful ex-governess, Baroness Lehzen, concluded from the mis-shapen body of the unfortunate Lady Flora that she was *enciente* and even a medical examination which proved them wrong, failed to scotch the scandal or to appease the Hastings family. The Queen, who had always mistrusted Lady Flora, did not realize that by listening to the malicious gossip of her ladies she had put herself into a false position and that the Tories were using the whole disgraceful business as a weapon in their political fight against the Whigs. Melbourne unwisely advised his royal mistress to do nothing, but when poor Lady Hastings died soon afterwards from a horrible liver complaint, the whole affair blew up again and the Queen was hissed by the Tory Duchess of Montrose and Lady Ingestre as she drove down the course at Ascot. Only her youth and inexperience could be put forward as an excuse for her conduct, which, in the eyes of Society, cast a slur upon the Court.

There were besides more important questions for the young Queen to consider than the squabbles among her ladies — above all the question of her marriage which had been proposed long before by her ubiquitous Uncle

2 Society ladies pay homage to the 18-year-old Queen, whose youth and freshness were combined with a natural grace and dignity. A. E. Chalon

Leopold, King of the Belgians. Her young cousin, Prince Albert of Saxe-Coburg and Gotha and his brother, Ernest, had already visited her at Kensington Palace in 1836 when she was still Princess Victoria, and she had enjoyed their company immensely in the very limited circle of acquaintance permitted by her mother's vigilance. Now everything was different, and the fear of having her new independence challenged by the need of deferring to a husband, however *gemütlich* he might be, upset her nerves and made her feel quite ill. She wrote to her Uncle in 1839 that she could make *'no final promise this year'*, underlining every word to emphasize her resolution and, in case he should overlook the seriousness of her feelings, adding that she had *'a great repugnance'* to the idea of changing her present situation.

She tried to postpone the Prince's visit arranged for the autumn and did succeed in putting it off for several days. But when he finally arrived at Windsor on 10 October at half-past seven in the evening and she stood at the top of the stairs to welcome him, she was instantly and completely overwhelmed. Albert was *beautiful!* 'Such beautiful blues eyes, an exquisite nose, such a pretty mouth with delicate mustachios and slight, but very slight whiskers.' A fairy tale Prince with a beautiful figure, 'broad in the shoulders and a fine waist'. A paragon! A demigod! Oh, how wonderful he looked! The Queen of England did not hesitate. She loved him from that moment until the day he died 20 years later and for 40 years after as his inconsolable widow.

The marriage took place on 10 February 1840 at the Chapel Royal, which was far too small to accommodate all the high-ranking guests who thought they should have been invited and were furiously indignant when they were not. Albert wore the uniform of a British Field-Marshal and the Order of the Garter and looked splendid. Yet in spite of this and the oath of naturalization he had sworn the day before the ceremony, in the eyes of the insular English aristocracy he was still a foreigner, a fact which further acquaintance with his character did nothing to diminish. His manner in society was formal and very correct. He was not a fox-hunting man – he preferred botany. He did not gamble or eat and drink to excess, or ogle the Maids of Honour. He was very high-minded and terribly stiff, with one peculiar relaxation that gave him pleasure – he liked playing the organ. 'How strange he is!' the Dowager Lady Lyttelton observed, hearing the sound of music 'expressively played by his master hand', as the sun was setting at Osborne. 'Such a modulation! Minor and solemn and ever changing ... from a *piano* up to the fullest swell.... And nobody but the organ knows what is in him, except indeed by the look in his eyes sometimes.'

Strange he certainly was and inexplicable, though not without influence on his doting Queen. For according to the ageing Duke of Wellington, it was not Victoria who was 'a great stickler for morality' at the beginning of her reign, it was Prince Albert who insisted on the character of the Court being spotless, 'the Queen not caring a straw about it' and the Prince being 'extremely strait-laced . . . whereas she was rather the other way.'

The Prince indeed was shocked by Victoria's giddy and headstrong behaviour. He did not share the pleasure she took in dancing all night and watching the dawn from the balcony at Buckingham Palace, which then had a splendid view of St Paul's. Late nights and too much gaiety upset his digestion; and coming from a small German principality that was far from rich, the extravagance of the Court appalled him. He believed in the dignity and splendour of the monarchy, not in the waste of money in the Queen's domestic arrangements; and at the risk of offending both political parties and the noblemen holding high office in the Royal Household, he produced a long memorandum revealing the absurdities of the system, or lack of system, that prevailed. The Lord Steward, he discovered, was responsible for laying the fires and the Lord Chamberlain for lighting them and as neither was properly represented at the Palace, the Queen was left to dine in a cold dining-room. The Master of the Household was not recognized by the Lord Chamberlain's office and consequently there was 'nobody to observe, correct, or to reprimand the male and female servants . . . if smoking, drinking and other irregularities occur in the dormitories' – a sad state of affairs, which the Prince cautiously and tactfully suggested could be improved if the Master of the Household ceased to be a political appointment and had full authority to reside in the Palace as the Lord Chamberlain's representative.

After some resistance from the Court officers and the staff at the Palace, these sensible recommendations were adopted. Not only was enough money saved for the Queen and her husband to invest in a country estate in the Isle of Wight, but a remarkable improvement was seen to have occurred in the organization of the entertainments at Buckingham Palace. When Her Majesty gave a state ball, the rooms, according to the *Illustrated London News*, were 'no longer crowded to such an excess as to conceal the display of beauty and destroy at once the freshness of the most brilliant *toilettes* and render the quadrille a scene of pressure and confusion, with only the semblance of dancing.' Instead the guests were marshalled into decorous groups according to precedence and 'the *coup d'oeil* was splendid, the contrast betwixt the *vaporeux* costumes of the youthful beauties and those of their dignified seniors striking and pleasing beyond description.'

The Queen and her handsome Prince opened the ball and danced until 11.15 p.m., when supper was served in the State Dining Room, resplendent with the gold candelabra and gold embossed flagons of the wicked Prince Regent, whose parties, as the Duke of Wellington remembered, often degenerated into a drunken rout with the ladies losing their shoes and a great deal besides and the gentlemen finishing up on the floor. Nothing like that happened now. There was no 'cornering', no 'squeezing and hugging' or improper behaviour. Further refreshments were served in Tippoo Sahib's Indian tent hung beneath the grand Corinthian portico beyond the Green Drawing-Room, and 'dancing was kept up with the subdued spirit, but with the more than ordinary gracefulness which characterizes royal balls' until, on the stroke of midnight, the band played 'God save the Queen' and the Prince firmly led Victoria away to their private apartments.

Some of the older, more raffish members of the aristocracy found the new régime too circumspect. Lord Stanley of Alderley thought the Court was 'dull and stupid', and 'with nothing to recommend it but virtue and respectability, it fell far below the calibre and character of good society.' Even the grand costume balls at Buckingham Palace, which cost £100,000 or more, were not always very enjoyable. The first, devised by Prince Albert to stimulate trade among the distressed silk weavers of Spitalfields, represented the medieval Court of King Edward III and Queen Philippa of Hainault, impersonated by himself and Victoria, who confessed to being quite bewildered by the Teutonic thoroughness of all the preparations. Mr Macready's wardrobe at Drury Lane Theatre was raided by the Duke of Wellington's sons in search of suits of armour, which made dancing somewhat uncomfortable, and the ladies found their wimples and tall hats rather hot. Richard Monckton Milnes, who fancied himself as a poet, went as Chaucer in 'a grave and simple suit of dark green cloth, amber satin and squirrel fur', which provoked the elderly Wordsworth to the observation that

3 A State Ball at Buckingham Palace in 1856. The crinoline, decorated with tiers of lace and tulle and wreaths of tiny flowers, was then the height of fashion and extremely flattering to the feminine figure

if Monckton Milnes went as Chaucer there was nothing left for him to do but to go as Monckton Milnes. In the end the medieval splendour and brilliance of the occasion did not come up to the aspiring young poet's expectations; he much preferred the less respectable society of the ageing Countess of Blessington at Gore House and the scalding wit of Lady Harriet Baring, whose parties at Bath House and the Grange in Hampshire were far more stimulating.

None the less attendance at Court was obligatory, both for the officers of state and their ladies and for any upper-class young man like Monckton Milnes ambitious to make his way in Society. And when the Season was over the Queen and Prince Albert left London to visit some of the grand country houses of the nobility. They stayed with the bachelor Duke of Devonshire at Chatsworth and admired the marvellous new glass conservatory his head gardener, Joseph Paxton, had built for him, the cascades and the fountains and the special illuminations put on for their enjoyment. They went to Belvoir as guests of the Duke of Rutland, and here the Prince took part in what he called 'a regular fox-hunt' among the fashionable hunting men of Melton and Leicester and astonished them all by keeping well up with the hounds. 'How well Albert's hunting answered!' the Queen exclaimed with pride and joy. 'It has made such a sensation.' And Albert himself spoke of their 'triumphant progress round the country' and the reception given to them by the populace. He was not apparently aware of the bad impression he created at Hatfield, where the 2nd Marquess of Salisbury made extensive preparations to receive the royal couple, redecorating a suite of rooms in crimson and gold and setting up splendid new entrance gates to the north front. The festivities included a grand ball for the local gentry, who could not fail to notice that the Prince was bored. 'He smiled at nobody; instead he stared restlessly about, now and again fixing his eyes on someone and whispering to the Queen. She was more affable, but joined in the whispering', which was not very complimentary to her host, who, like his ancestor Robert Cecil, Lord Treasurer to Queen Elizabeth I, had spared no expense on her entertainment.

The Marquess, who could be very choleric when roused, declined to comment on his guest's lack of courtesy. With the Great Hall at Hatfield hung with portraits of Queen Elizabeth, Lord Burleigh and all the Cecils from father to son down the generations, and the armoury with trophies salvaged from the Armada, the sullen behaviour of a haughty German princeling was not of any great importance. Even the Queen herself with her Hanoverian descent was something of an upstart compared with the Englishness of the Cecils, whose ancestry and long tradition of service to the realm endowed them with a power and privilege they accepted without snobbery or conceit and used discreetly. They had no need to seek favour from the Sovereign or to bend the knee to her stiff Teutonic husband.

But the Queen was so enamoured of her Prince, she put Society in the wrong for failing to appreciate him, and since his taste lay in the direction of a quiet domestic life 'away from all the bitterness people create for themselves

20

in London', she was soon dilating on the joys of her own country house at Osborne. The Prince himself designed it in the style of a large Italian villa, with the help of Thomas Cubitt, the architect of Belgravia; and he filled it with rows of heavy Germanic busts in bronze set in recesses crowned with gilded plaster shells, with pseudo-classical marble figures and marble reproductions of the hands and feet of his wife and children, and with huge pieces of 'modern' furniture decorated in a Gothic style more suitable to the medieval town of Coburg than to a private residence in the Isle of Wight. Charles Greville thought the house was 'very ugly'; Lady Charlotte Canning found it comfortable and admired the splendid views of the hills and the sea and said she had never seen the royal couple looking so happy 'with their babes around them'.

Osborne, however, was a mere *bagatelle* to Prince Albert's next adventure in architecture in the Highlands of Scotland, where the glorious, icy cold air and the wild countryside reminded him of his native Thuringia. At Balmoral all his latent gifts as a designer were poured into the creation of a romantic baronial castle, more Scottish than any Scotsman would ever have thought possible. Built in granite, the exterior, with a multitude of turrets puncturing the sky, frowned above the River Dee, and the interior rambled through a series of immense rooms and long corridors that fought a losing battle with the stoves intended to heat them. Everything that could be covered in tartan was. There were tartan carpets on the floor, tartan curtains and chair covers with frills of the Balmoral tartan in red and grey, the Victoria tartan with a white stripe and the Royal Stuart tartan of the Queen's distant forbears. She thought it was all 'utterly *beautiful!*' 'Every year,' she wrote, 'my heart becomes more fixed in this dear paradise, and so much more so now, that all has become my dear Albert's own creation, own work, own building ... and his great taste and the impress of his dear hand have been stamped everywhere.' If she heard that some people at Court spoke of 'tartanitis' she ignored it, that was just another thoughtless jibe by the *beau monde* jealous of Albert's superior taste and wisdom.

4 Queen Victoria and Prince Albert in 1854 on the 14th anniversary of their marriage. The bewhiskered Prince was never less than perfect in the Queen's sight; she adored him. Photographed by Roger Fenton

Both Charles Greville, Clerk to the Privy Council, and Lord John Russell, the Whig statesman, while staying at Balmoral, found the Prince more relaxed and approachable in his Scottish retreat than he ever was in London. He came into the breakfast room and sat down with them and 'seemed very much at his ease, very gay, pleasant and without the least stiffness or air of dignity.' Another visitor, Sir Charles Lyell, also observed that 'his nature expanded and became simplified and the hauteur in which he so often surrounded himself was banished' as soon as he donned a kilt. But his sporting activities, though a capital subject for the brush of his favourite painter, Sir Edwin Landseer, met with a good deal of hostility from his Scottish neighbours, since he was a poor shot and preferred the unsporting, Teutonic *battue*, where the birds and beasts were driven towards the guns to be slaughtered, to the more haphazard chances of deer-stalking or going out on the moors with a gun and a dog.

The trouble was that he made no attempt to adapt himself to the country of his adoption. Constantly exhorted by his ex-tutor and friend, Baron Stockmar, 'to cleave devoutly and unceasingly to high thoughts and noble purposes', he believed it was his duty to reform the easy-going habits of the landed gentry, whose belief in themselves and their way of life belonged to the traditions of a long history he failed to understand. When he watched the

5 The Grand Staircase at Buckingham Palace, designed by John Nash made a splendid setting for the aristocratic guests on a ball night in 1848. Eugene Lami

boys at Eton playing cricket, he suggested that those in the field would be better employed jumping up and down as a healthy exercise instead of waiting for the ball to come their way. He did not realize that the game had become a sacred upper-class ritual ever since Lord John Sackville and his head gardener at Knole had played together on the village green in the eighteenth century; nor did he understand that cricket had a moral and civilizing influence over a generation whose parents and grandparents had indulged in cock-fighting, bear-baiting and pugilism. He had not heard that the Battle of Waterloo was said to have been won on the playing-fields of Eton — the statement would have mystified him if he had; and it was not surprising if the Eton boys dubbed him a prig, resenting his interference and his lack of humour and rejoicing when he ruined a new pair of lavender kid gloves while laying a foundation stone for a new building at the school. Accustomed to all sorts of eccentricities in their aristocratic parents, their own friends and the masters who flogged them without much mercy, they were not prepared to accept a foreigner with pale blue eyes and a haughty stare who thought he could teach them how to play cricket.

Their elders found this didactic spirit in the Prince even more tiresome, mistrusting his intellectual superiority and his powers of reasoning, and so the rift between the respectable Court and smart Society widened as time went on. Even the Great Exhibition of 1851, which was a fantastic success and Prince Albert's greatest achievement, did not meet with much approbation from the upper classes. 'I believe it is quite universally sneered at by the *beau monde*, and will only increase the contempt for the Prince among all fine folk,' the Dowager Lady Lyttelton wrote, adding rather sadly, since she was one of his warmest admirers: 'But so would anything he does.'

6 The Queen and Prince Albert in the Highlands of Scotland, where they enjoyed 'the simple life' and the Prince went stag hunting and fishing like a country gentleman. Sir Edwin Landseer R.A.

A barrage of criticism from all sides had met the Prince from the very beginning of the proceedings, especially from *The Times* and from Colonel Sibthorp, the Member of Parliament for Lincoln. 'The project looks so like insanity,' *The Times* declared, 'that we can scarcely bring ourselves to believe that the advisers of the Prince have dared to connect his name with such an outrage to the feelings and wishes of the inhabitants of the metropolis.' And Colonel Sibthorp went even further. 'As for the object for which Hyde Park is to be desecrated, it is the greatest trash, the greatest fraud and the greatest imposition ever to be palmed upon the people of this country,' he cried, adding that every species of fraud and immorality would be practised by the bad characters attracted to the Exhibition.

He was wrong. The huge parties of people from the 'industrial classes', who came by excursion train from all parts of the country and were guided by 'some leader a little higher in station than themselves', behaved in the most exemplary fashion, perhaps because the Prince decreed that no beer or alcohol was to be served in the refreshment rooms, only filtered water and lemonade. And the opening day with the sun shining on Paxton's glittering Crystal Palace was a triumph. The Queen and the Prince drove to Hyde Park in a procession of state landaus, with their two eldest children, the Princess Victoria and the Prince of Wales, and were met by a deputation of gentlemen who had served on the committee, a flourish of trumpets and the national anthem. The Archbishop of Canterbury, the Prime Minister, Lord John Russell, the elderly Duke of Wellington, leaning on the arm of Lord

7 A royal tour of the Great Exhibition of 1851 in Paxton's magical Crystal Palace, where 'myriads of wonderful things' were on show and the Queen went into raptures of delight because it was a triumphant success for Prince Albert

Anglesey, and a host of other important people joined the procession up the nave to the royal dais by the Crystal Fountain. Even the '*soi-disant* fashionables' the Queen disliked so much were there, though they did not go to look at this Great Exhibition of the arts and industries of the world; they went to be seen and to see each other, or because the Lord Chamberlain had commanded them and they could not very well refuse.

Thackeray, by then as Charlotte Brontë somewhat spitefully noted, 'the pet and darling of high society', was invited and thought 'it was a noble awful great love inspiring goose flesh bringing sight ... the general effect, the multitude, the riches, the peace, the splendour ... much grander than a coronation.' And the Queen herself was in ecstasies. The tremendous cheering, the joy expressed in every face, the vastness of the building, the sound of the organ and the *Hallelujah* chorus sung by the choir of 600 voices moved her deeply, and especially because it was all her beloved Albert's doing and at last, as she told Lord Granville, she felt 'dearest Albert *was now* appreciated by everyone.'

The Queen wore a diamond diadem with a little crown at the back and two feathers, a pink and silver dress with a full skirt and a lace fichu draped in folds over her bosom. This charming fashion of the 1850s suited her admirably, for at the age of 32 she was already the mother of seven children and the plump young girl who had danced all night at Buckingham Palace, had matured into a highly respectable, dumpy little woman with a regal air of grace and dignity. Pink seemed to be her favourite colour—it showed off her diamonds splendidly. But in 1843 when she visited Louis Philippe at the Chateau d'Eu, she appeared in a very unbecoming shade of cerise, which disagreed violently with her complexion and according to Lady Charlotte Canning, 'made her look very hot'.

State occasions, with great balls and banquets in the Waterloo Chamber at Windsor and the new Music Room at Buckingham Palace, obliged the Queen to take an interest in fashion, though not in its more frivolous aspects. She never ordered a gown or a bonnet without asking her husband's advice and perhaps his advice was not always for the best, for her gowns tended to be rich and fussy and her taste for bright colours, gay ribbons and frills of lace was often ridiculed by the *soi-disant* fashionables. The Duchess of Sutherland, the Duchess of Bedford and the Duchess of Buccleuch had little difficulty in outshining her and their family jewels were as brilliant as those belonging to the Crown, while the Marchioness of Douro, wife of the Duke of Wellington's eldest son, had a tall and stately elegance the Queen sometimes envied. If Albert had not so disliked the society of women, the competition to attract him might have been keener and the Queen more anxious. As it was she had no need to fear. He was immune to temptation.

Yet the quiet domesticity of the royal couple was not without its tempestuous moments. Although the dowager Lady Lyttelton admired the Prince for his 'candour, truth, prudence and manliness' and thought the Queen's 'wifely submission to him' was exactly as it should be, there were frequent storms when the vigorous young Queen lost control of her temper and became as unreasonable as the Prince Regent in the heyday of his self-indulgent youth. Albert's efforts to calm her were not always successful. When he tried to reason with her, she became more, not less excitable, and when he walked away into another room, she ran after him 'to have it all out', which meant yet another painful, emotional scene, especially when her nerves were upset by her frequent pregnancies.

Contrary to the public image that so impressed the nation and the middle classes in particular, the Queen was not by any means a maternal woman. 'You cannot *really* wish me to be the *"mamma d'une nombreuse famille"*', she wrote to her Uncle Leopold after the birth of her first child, Princess Victoria. 'Men never think, at least seldom think, what a hard task it is for us to go through this *very* often.' And to that same daughter after she had married the Crown Prince of Prussia and was expecting her first baby, she wrote with a quite extraordinary down-to-earth candour: 'What you say of the pride of giving life to an immortal soul is very fine, dear, but I own I cannot enter into that; I think much more of our being like a cow or a dog at such moments when our poor nature becomes so very animal and unecstatic.' It had, she confessed made her 'miserable' to have the first two years of her married life 'utterly spoilt' by this occupation. 'I could enjoy nothing,' she complained, 'not travel about or go about with dear Papa', and if only she had 'waited a year', she believed things would have been 'very different'.

This sentiment could well have been echoed by many an innocent bride, who, after all the fun and festivity of her wedding, was abandoned to the conjugal demands of her husband and only really became interesting to her in-laws when she showed signs of producing an heir. For the landed gentry believed in family continuity and primogeniture was their gospel. Whether or not the wife loved her husband or wanted children was quite incidental. Indeed love as a motive for marriage was deeply mistrusted—at least by one forthright *grande dame*, the Hon. Catherine Neville, a sister of Lady Glynne, who wrote to her charming niece, Mary, when she had refused an eligible suitor: 'Women are not like men. They cannot chuse [sic], nor is it creditable or lady-like to be "what is called in love". I believe that very few regulated minds have ever been and that romantic attachment is confined to *novels* and novel readers, ye silly and numerous class of idle young persons ill-educated at home or in Boarding Schools.' Mary, as it happened, was neither silly nor idle and she did love George Lyttelton, the man she eventually married; but the twelfth child she uncomplainingly gave birth to during the 17 years of her married life, killed her.

Fortunately the Queen was physically very strong indeed. She retained her vitality, her resilience and her obstinacy through all the crises of her married life and even when she quarrelled with the Prince, he was never less than perfect in her eyes. She depended on him utterly. His desk with a green shaded lamp above it stood next to hers, piled high with Cabinet papers and state documents, and she had absolute faith in his judgment. He drafted all her letters, wrote her dispatches and analysed the political problems of each day in the long memoranda that poured from his pen; and it was in this sphere of activity that he at last made some headway against the underlying hostility of the aristocratic governing class.

At first his domination of the Queen was viewed with the utmost suspicion and especially his interference in foreign affairs, where his bias towards Germany was fraught with dangerous possibilities. It was all very well when he concerned himself with the arts and sciences, presiding over committees to discuss the frescoes for the new Houses of Parliament and the pursuit of scientific knowledge in the coal-mines; but as soon as he started to dabble in diplomacy, he came up against Lord Palmerston, who had already spent half a life-time in politics and knew more about the ins and outs of every court and cabinet in Europe than any other living creature.

Palmerston was the very antithesis of the Prince: bold, amorous and instinctive; a gay, ambitious, self-confident English milord, with a genius for guiding the ship of state through stormy waters. As a young Regency buck he had waltzed with the Countess of Lieven at Almack's, the most exclusive club in London, and had earned the name of 'Cupid' for his many love affairs. But he was devoted to Lord Melbourne's beautiful sister, Lady Cowper, and when her husband died in 1837, he urged her to marry him. Society thought it was quite ridiculous. She was 52 and a grandmother and he was 55, yet 'so completely happy it was a pleasure to look at him' and so enthralled by his lovely wife, their marriage in 1839 lasted blissfully until the day of his death 26 years later.

Such a man could be forgiven if he believed that his long experience at the Foreign Office was more useful than the carefully considered opinions of a young German prince trained in the academies of Brussels and Bonn. He ran the Foreign Office in his own way—a very English way, which appeared to be quite haphazard—taking risks that put the fear of God into some of his Cabinet colleagues and acting on his own responsibility with a bland self-assurance that increased his popularity as a public figure, but appalled the Queen and her husband. The Queen complained that dispatches in her name were sent to foreign governments before she had seen them. She nagged the Prime Minister, Lord John Russell, and lectured his Cabinet colleague, Lord Clarendon after a private dinner at Windsor. Albert wrote a long memorandum on what was expected of the Foreign Secretary and Palmerston apologized. He agreed to be more circumspect in the future—and went on exactly as before.

The Queen and the Prince in their fury decided that such arrogant, slap-dash behaviour could not be permitted. Palmerston must be dismissed—and in 1851, Palmerston was dismissed on the flimsy charge that in conversation with the French Ambassador, he had committed the Government to a full and unqualified approval of Prince Louis Napoleon's *coup d'état* without consulting the Cabinet first.

'Palmerston is out!' Greville exclaimed and the Court rejoiced. But Palmerston could cut a parliamentary opponent down to size with the scarifying brilliance of his oratory and, a week later, dine with him or meet him in the hunting-field without rancour. Nothing—not even the loss of the Foreign

8 Lord Palmerston, Foreign Secretary and Prime Minister: a self-confident, buccaneering English mi-lord with a genius for conducting the ship of state through stormy waters. F. Cruickshank

Office—could destroy his 'jaunty step' or the extraordinary vigour of his personality. And so it was that the man Lord John Russell had told the Queen in 1851 'was too old to do much in the future', made an unexpected come-back four years later when the nation had plunged into the Crimean War and was in dire distress at the muddle and misconduct of its affairs.

Palmerston became Prime Minister because the English people had faith in his courage and his determination, and with one short interval he remained Prime Minister for the next ten years, strangely enough working in close co-operation with the Crown. What might have been a Quixotic situation fraught with misunderstandings developed instead into one of mutual respect; for now the Prince and the Prime Minister were drawn together by their hostility towards Russia and the ebullient English milord discovered that the Teutonic thoroughness of the dyspeptic Prince had its virtues. His recommendations on the conduct of the war were valuable, clear and efficient, each long memorandum closely reasoned and worthy of consideration. And Palmerston was far too generous to bear a grudge against his ex-adversary. He extolled the capabilities of the Prince and persuaded his colleagues in the Cabinet to look on him with greater favour.

But Albert, designated Prince Consort by letters patent published by the Crown in 1857 and King in all but name, was never to become popular in Society. Etiquette at Court remained stiff and cold. No one, not even the Duchess of Sutherland as Mistress of the Robes, was ever invited to sit down in the royal box when Victoria and Albert attended the opera, and all the Queen's ladies had to put up with standing on their feet for hours on end in the draughty corridors at Balmoral or the drawing-rooms of Windsor and Buckingham Palace. Abroad, when visiting the King of the Belgians and the Coburg Court of the Prince's father and brother, intolerable complications in matters of precedence arose for the Queen's Lady-in-Waiting, Lady Charlotte Canning, and Lord Aberdeen as the Minister in Attendance. And all this, it was felt, was due to the Prince's unbending character. He never relaxed, even in masculine company. He refused to dally over the port after dinner and was not interested in swapping stories about hunting and shooting, or in scandal and sex. He had been taught that the English aristocracy were flippant, immoral and obsessed with the idea of their own superiority, and he believed it. Their society bored him and he took no pains to conceal the fact.

It was only at home with his children that the Prince unbent, with his adored eldest daughter, Vicky, and the younger children, but not with his eldest son, Bertie. The Prince of Wales was more of a Hanoverian than a Coburg: affectionate, pleasure-loving, not at all intellectual and given to uncontrollable spasms of rage. Neither of his parents made the slightest attempt to understand him and their efforts to mould him into a super imitation of his father were disastrous. He was encumbered with middle-aged tutors, hemmed in by strict rules of conduct, forced to study until his exhausted and bewildered brain could go no farther and not allowed out into Society at the age of 18 without being surrounded by a horde of spies. It was hardly surprising if, at the first opportunity that ever came his way, in camp with the Guards at Curragh, he delighted in the comely shape of the actress Nellie Clifden who was smuggled into his tent by one of his brother officers.

For Prince Albert this was the most humiliating indignity the flippant Society of his adopted country could have thought of casting upon him. He was utterly horrified and bitterly disappointed. The Queen said she would never forget the look on his face when he first heard about his son's escapade and what was worse, she blamed this very natural episode in her son's life for the calamity which so soon afterwards swept the ground from under her feet.

The Prince was no longer handsome. At 42 he was bald and flabby, over-

burdened by his obsession for work, tired-looking and prematurely aged. He suffered from rheumatism, insomnia and depression; and when he was taken ill in November 1861 with a fever that Sir James Clark failed to diagnose as typhoid, almost everyone, except the Queen, realized he was a dying man.

For days on end she obstinately refused to believe the evidence of her own eyes and was furious with Lord Palmerston for suggesting that another doctor should be called in. The death of her beloved husband was inconceivable. She simply could not and would not consider the possibility. Yet even the Queen of England with her plump and powerful little hands could not push the ugly monster of death away.

She had written after the demise of her brother-in-law that she thought it was 'positively wrong to dislike mourning,' adding that 'darling Beatrice', her three-year-old daughter, looked 'lovely in her black silk and crepe dress.' Now, throughout the corridors of Windsor Castle, sewing maids, tailors and members of the Household busied themselves quietly with the preparations that were necessary to plunge the Court into darkness. The staff of the famous Mourning Warehouse in Regent Street, established by Mr W. C. Jay in 1841, more expert in the arcane mysteries of black crepe, black paramatta, black bombazine, black printed muslins and black jet trimmings of bugles and beads, worked round the clock—Mr Jay was not the man to be caught napping. And on the night of 14 December, the Prince died.

'Two or three long but perfectly gentle breaths were drawn,' the Queen wrote in her Journal, 'the hand clasping mine and ... *all, all* was over.' Lady Augusta Bruce, the Duchess of Sutherland and Sir Charles Phipps could do nothing. They led the Queen away and laid her on a sofa in the Red Room. She was a widow now and for ever. The brightness of the day had gone, the gloom of the night had come. And although she resolved never to be found wanting in her sovereign duty to her country, she withdrew altogether from Society and never allowed her Court to go out of mourning.

Some men—Lord Palmerston, Disraeli and the Duke of Argyll—paid high tribute to her late husband. Others did not. The Earl of Orford rudely remarked: 'That, at least, is one foreigner out of the way', and he deliberately put on a pair of light check trousers he had been keeping especially for the occasion, for as Lord Lennox said to Sir Henry Cole: 'Truth to say the "Swells" as a class did not much like the Prince.' Yet the Prince by dominating the Queen and the Court had influenced the upper classes more deeply than they themselves realized. By the time he died many of the worldly aristocratic families had accepted a code of conduct that was more earnest, more godly and more virtuous than that of their extravagant forbears and, if only for the sake of their own survival in a changing world, had learnt to behave with greater circumspection. The solemn obsequies of the Prince's funeral were a fitting conclusion to a life spent in so much endeavour to improve the moral tone of his adopted country.

9 The last hours of Prince Albert in December 1861. His death plunged the grief-stricken Queen into mourning for the rest of her long life. 'There is no one *now* to call me Victoria ... the world has gone for *me*!'

10 The sombre and magnificent funeral procession of Prince Albert, the pall-bearers wearing top hats sashed with 'weepers' and the hearse plumed with black ostrich feathers

2
The Aristocracy at Home

An American visitor to England in the early nineteenth century, more sympathetic towards the aristocracy than the German Prince Consort, observed that 'the permanent interests and affections of the most opulent classes here centre almost universally in the country. They have *houses* in London, in which they stay while Parliament sits and occasionally visit at other seasons; but their homes are in the country ... where they flourish in pomp and joy.' And this was absolutely true.

The great landscape gardeners and architects of the eighteenth century, working with their noble patrons, had created palaces and parks in the English countryside, which for elegance and beauty had never been surpassed by any other nation. Peacocks paced the terraces at Blenheim, deer browsed in the shade of the trees at Woburn, cascades and fountains flashed in the sunshine at Chatsworth, and for miles around the rich agricultural land, green pastures and woodlands stretched as far as the eye could see. Villages and farms owing their allegiance to the territorial grandees, nestled round ancient churches, where the ancestral tombs of the family were a witness to the continuity of their ownership from the days of the crusading knights lying in suits of marble armour beside their wives and children and with a favourite basset hound at their feet.

A great deal of change from one generation to the next had been absorbed by a gradual process of peaceful evolution; for the patrician landlords had a progressive outlook and a mania for the 'improvement' of their estates and, unlike the French *noblesse* across the Channel, they were seldom absentees from choice, only when the business of the state called them away from the country life they prized so highly. In local affairs their word was law, and through their patronage of the Church with the livings at their disposal and their control of the parliamentary seats in their extensive domain, their influence extended to embrace the whole government of the United Kingdom. Their eldest sons sat in the House of Commons before coming into their inheritance and moving on to the House of Lords. Their younger sons entered the Church, the diplomatic service or the armed forces. But always the focus of their lives was at home in the country with their horses and their dogs, their guns and their fishing-rods, among the innumerable retainers, whose loyal service guaranteed the leisure and pleasure they enjoyed.

Even with the dramatic and bewildering developments of the Industrial Revolution, which in time were to change the whole balance of society, the territorial magnates continued 'to flourish in pomp and joy'. Many of them acquired new wealth from the exploitation of the mineral resources of their land and the huge sums of money they received from the railway companies of the 1840s, who were obliged by law to pay compensation to the landowners for every inch of ground to be covered by a new route passing across their property. The Duke of Rutland had mining interests in Leicestershire and the Duke of Devonshire owned 186,000 acres of Derbyshire and Yorkshire rich in coal and iron. The Duke of Bedford enjoyed an income of £120,000 a year from his agricultural estates and as much again from his property in London which had been developed in the eighteenth century. The Earl of Derby, a direct descendant of the 1st Earl who had been created after the Battle of Bosworth in 1485, besides owning some 70,000 acres of agricultural land in Lancashire and Cheshire worth £150,000 a year, had property in Liverpool, Manchester, Preston, Blackburn, Bolton and other towns of the Midlands and the North which the expansion of industry made increasingly profitable.

While some of the big estates had been seriously damaged by the idle, extravagant behaviour of the generation that had grown up with the Prince Regent, most of this great wealth was settled by entail on the eldest son and his heirs and therefore untouchable; and even before Queen Victoria ascended the throne in 1837, a reaction had set in among the younger members of the aristocracy against the immorality and frivolity of their immediate predecessors. The 6th Duke of Devonshire, who inherited Chatsworth in 1811 at the age of 21, had seen his mother, the ravishingly beautiful Duchess Georgiana, destroyed by her fatal addiction to gambling at whist and faro, and he had grown up in the explosive *ménage à trois* at Devonshire House where his father's mistress and his mother's dearest friend, Lady Elizabeth Foster, and her brood of illegitimate children had all been part of the household. Perhaps that was why he never married, dying a bachelor in 1858. He was eligible enough—rich, sweet-tempered, kind and affectionate, though rather deaf from childhood—and hunted like a stag by every high-born mother with marriageable daughters. Or perhaps he was too absorbed in Chatsworth and all its treasures, in the library he bought from the Bishop of Ely and the collection of rare coins and medals which cost him a cool £50,000. He declined most of the public appointments that were offered to him, preferring the company of his head gardener, Joseph Paxton, who created the immense glass Conservatory at Chatsworth and the Lily House for the giant water lily *Victoria Regia,* that first bloomed with great splendour in 1849 and brought the Duke hurrying home from Ireland to celebrate his gardener's success.

Not everyone approved of the Duke's very close and intimate relationship with Paxton, for as Queen Victoria kept on reminding everyone after she had knighted him for his work on the Crystal Palace, 'he *was* only an ordinary gardener's boy.' The Duke, however, paid no attention to the lack of birth and breeding in his protegé and took no notice when his sister, Lady Granville, complained half-jokingly of 'you and your Paxton sitting under a red rhododendron at Chatsworth ... and with no thought of your country's weal or woe.' He treated his gardener as a friend and trusted him implicitly.

Paxton organized all the entertainments at Chatsworth and the brilliant fête at the Duke's Palladian villa in Middlesex, given in honour of the Tsar of Russia in the summer of 1844. All the élite of London drove out to Chiswick in their carriages for this dazzling event, the Duke of Sutherland, the Duchess of Beaufort, the Marquess of Londonderry, the Marquess of Lansdowne and many others ostentatiously attended by outriders in livery, and the Viscountess Pollington daringly driving herself in a smart equipage drawn by two black Orloff ponies, which were much admired. Two splendid bands of the Royal Horse Guards and the Coldstream Guards were drawn up on the lawn to welcome the visitors and a captain's guard of the 17th Lancers escorted the carriage containing the Emperor, Prince Albert and the King of Saxony.

The Emperor wore a dark blue dress coat with yellow buttons and a star and though his heavy-lidded eyes and olive skinned complexion gave him an exotic apperance, his manner was very affable as he held court in the circular Salon of the villa. The party then adjourned for a *déjeuner* in the

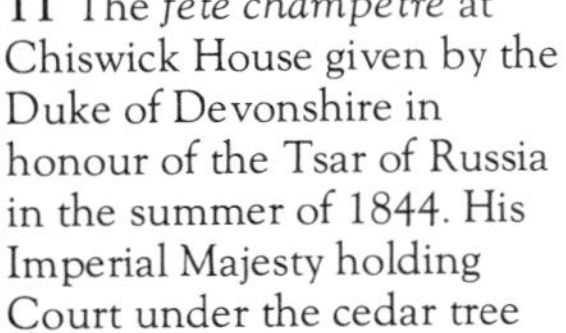

11 The *fête champêtre* at Chiswick House given by the Duke of Devonshire in honour of the Tsar of Russia in the summer of 1844. His Imperial Majesty holding Court under the cedar tree

Summer Parlour, which had been draped with cream-coloured silk embroidered with the Tsar's emblem in black and gold, Queen Victoria's Royal Coat of Arms and the heraldic device of the Cavendish family. 'The dressing of the table was extremely chaste,' wrote the *Illustrated London News* reporter. 'Silver plate only was used, the larger and more richly chased standard pieces being filled with fruit (the hot-house wonders of Chatsworth) and groups of flowers, which had a charming classic effect. We have seen several noble banquets, but we have never witnessed any appointments that evinced such refined taste or were, in themselves, so unexceptionably beautiful. "Flowers and silver" say we, in spite of all the temptations to exhibit gold, are the fit decoration for a *fête champêtre.*' Footmen clad in the rich yellow state livery of the ducal household served the delectable meal and afterwards the guests wandered into the spacious garden to watch His Imperial Majesty plant a tree and to inspect the giraffes, which, as a gift to the Emperor, had been brought to Chiswick from the Surrey Zoological Gardens before being shipped to St Petersburg.

The Duke of Devonshire also entertained on a princely scale at Chatsworth. 'Forty people sat down to dinner every day,' Greville reported of one house party, 'and about 150 servants in the Steward's Room and Servants' Hall. Nothing could be more agreeable from the gaiety of numbers and the entire liberty that prevails; all the resources of the house—horses, carriages, keepers etc—are placed at the disposal of the guests and everyone does what they like best. In the evening they acted charades or danced, and there was plenty of whist and ecarté high and low.'

Such lavish house parties were a feature of life in most of the great country houses, the guests often staying for several weeks in the hunting and shooting season to enjoy the generous hospitality of their hosts. At Belvoir Castle on the Duke of Rutland's birthday, an immense party assembled for the ball opened by the Duke with the Duchess of Sutherland, who, according to Greville, had to 'sail down at least a hundred couple of Tenants, shopkeepers, valets and Abigails', since the feasting and the fun was not confined to the Duke and his high-ranking guests. The whole Vale of Belvoir rang with chiming bells as the tenants and villagers made merry on the beef and ale distributed among them by their noble master.

'I should like to bring the surly Radical here who scowls and snarls at the selfish aristocracy who have no sympathies with the people,' Greville wrote, adding: 'The Duke of Rutland is as selfish as any man of his class—that is, he never does what he does not like, and spends his whole life in a round of such pleasures as suit his taste, but he is neither a foolish nor a bad man, and partly from a sense of duty, partly from inclination, he devotes his time and labour to the interest and welfare of the people who live and labour on his estate.' He regularly attended the meetings of the Poor Law Guardians and visited the people in need of assistance in their own homes, sitting and talking to them with more genuine sympathy, Greville thought, than any Radical with his high-falutin', abstract political theories of destroying the rich to benefit the poor.

As Lord Lieutenant of the county, the Duke was respected and very highly esteemed, and as Master of the Fox Hounds popular with everyone. The whole neighbourhood, rich and poor alike, turned out when the meet was at Belvoir Castle to watch the hunt servants in their smart livery, the eager, jostling hounds and the superbly glossy horses groomed and saddled to perfection. For hunting, if the Prince Consort had only realized it, was not just a sport enjoyed by the privileged aristocracy; it was a celebration which drew the country people together into a single community. The farmer mounted on his cob, the squire, the parson and the villagers on foot all loved the spectacle of the hounds streaming across the open country on a cold winter's morning with the field galloping after them, and when the hunt returned exhausted and muddy after a long run, all the talk in the neighbourhood was of the day's sport.

Nevertheless it cost a fortune to keep up the stables and kennels attached to a big house and not all the great estates recovered very quickly from the excesses of the Regency generation. At Blenheim, in 1857, the 7th Duke of Marlborough inherited the accumulated debts of his father and his spendthrift grandfather as well as the enormous palace built by Vanbrugh for the 1st Duke and his quarrelsome Duchess Sarah. He had two sons and six daughters and a large number of dependents for whom he felt it was his duty to provide; for unlike his extravagant predecessors, he was sober in his tastes and very serious. As a young man, while studying at Oxford, he had absorbed the ideals of the High Church Tractarian Movement, which under the leadership of John Keble, Edward Pusey and John Henry Newman had stimulated a revival of Anglo-Catholicism within the established Church. The Tractarians believed in ceremony, in confession, incense burning and many of the rites belonging to the Church of Rome and were accused of 'Popery' by the fiercely Protestant Evangelicals or Low Churchmen; but their influence spread and all through his life, the principles of the Oxford Movement continued to inspire the Duke of Marlborough with a steady devotion.

His Duchess, the eldest daughter of the Marquess of Londonderry, was described as 'a woman of remarkable character and capacity, judicious and tactful', which no doubt she had to be to run such a large household on £5,000 a year. But rather a different view of her was taken by her American daughter-in-law, Lady Randolph Churchill, who found the immense palace with its high ceilings and vast rooms oppressive and the Duchess hard to please. No one dared to do anything without her permission and every moment of the day was mapped out from the ceremonial breakfast preceded by family prayers to the formal, full dress dinner in the cold dining-room.

The morning was taken up with studying the newspapers, writing letters and for Jennie, practising the piano with Lord Randolph's sister. At luncheon the Duke and Duchess carved the joints of meat and the younger children filled baskets with food from the table to distribute later to the poor and the sick cottagers on the estate. A drive in the afternoon to visit some of the neighbours, or a walk in the gardens, was followed by tea at 5 o'clock with

12 *Left* The 7th Duke of Marlborough, who inherited Blenheim Palace in 1857: a sober and serious-minded aristocrat, devoted to the interests of the Church, his family and the welfare of his tenants

13 *Right* The Duchess of Marlborough: a proud woman of remarkable character and capacity, whose strict and inflexible regime at Blenheim had to be obeyed by everyone

the Duchess presiding until the moment when she invariably announced to all the ladies present that she was sure they needed 'a little rest', whereupon they were able to escape to their own rooms until it was time to dress for dinner. This was a very solemn affair, according to Jennie, and there was no escape afterwards from sitting around in the Van Dyck Room until the clock chimed 11.0. and the bedroom candles were lit for the company to take upstairs after kissing the Duke and Duchess good-night.

There were occasions, however, when the Marlboroughs felt it was their duty to entertain in the grand manner. In 1859, when the young Prince of Wales was in residence at Oxford, they gave a ball in his honour, although it was called 'an evening party' as this description sounded less frivolous. The ball was preceded by a dinner party, the guests gathering in one of the drawing-rooms and walking in procession through one room after another to the stately Grand Saloon, which was brilliantly illuminated by gas and candle-light. Mrs Jeune, wife of the Master of Pembroke College, was dazzled by the gold plate on the table, the diamond necklace worn by the Duchess, Lady Macclesfield's glittering tiara as high as a fender and the shoulder knots of rubies and diamonds on the wife of the Austrian Ambassador. She thought, when the dancing began in two of the Tapestry Rooms, that 'some of the Oxford people roamed around looking somewhat disconsolate', but her two daughters, Margaret and Lydia, were not overawed by their surroundings and the young Prince danced 'every dance of every kind' with zest and good humour.

Later the Prince returned to Blenheim for a shooting party and the celebrations in the evening were described by a local newspaper as 'the most brilliant spectacle in the county for a century.' Three hundred people were entertained to a banquet and all the apartments along the south front of the Palace blazed with lights, so that the hundreds of spectators allowed into the grounds for the evening could watch the guests enjoying themselves.

After all this it was not surprising that the Duchess of Marlborough went into 'hysterics of rage and mortification' when she received no invitation to the wedding of the Prince of Wales and Princess Alexandra in 1865, or that the Duke, badly in need of money, had to sell one of the chief treasures of Blenheim, the unique collection of antique gems formed by the 4th Duke in the eighteenth century. Unhappily this sale, which realized 30,000 guineas, failed to resolve the Duke's financial difficulties, and by finding some loophole in the Blenheim Settled Estate Act, he later sold the famous Sunderland Library and opened the way for his eldest son to make a clean sweep in 1886 of the Van Dycks, the Rembrandts and the large paintings by Rubens.

Aesthetically, the taste of the Victorian upper clases left a good deal to be desired. The Marlboroughs never looked at the superb pictures hanging on the walls at Blenheim—they had been there ever since anyone could remember and were taken for granted, though the voluptuous contours of the ladies painted by Rubens may have been a little disturbing to the minds of the exceedingly moral Duke and Duchess. Elsewhere, other richer members of the aristocracy developed a passion for opulent ornamentation, and dissatisfied with their ancestors' more restrained mode of decoration, revamped their houses in a variety of styles.

In 1860, the 4th Marquess of Bath tore the interior of Longleat to pieces and inspired by the Italian Renaissance, entirely redecorated the suite of rooms on the east side of the house. Designs taken from the Ducal Palace in Venice were copied or adapted and Italian craftsmen brought over to Wiltshire to execute the highly skilled work on the ceilings, which were soon overloaded with imitation Veroneses, Titians and Tiepolos, set in square and circular panels and elaborate mouldings painted in strong colours. In the Saloon, originally the Long Gallery of the Elizabethan house, the proud Marquess inserted a gigantic marble chimneypiece, crowded with exuberantly carved figures and supported by naked Atlases, seemingly bowed down by the weight of the mantelpiece on top of their bent heads. Panels representing *War, Land and Sea Power, Poetry* and *Music,* were fitted into the walls between huge Flemish tapestries, the door frames surrounded by alabaster and the doorknobs furnished in gilt. Specially woven carpets, ebony and ormolu cabinets, brocaded chairs, gilded clocks and Meissen figures of animals and birds completed the garish effect, which pleased the Marquess so much, he placed a tablet above the window recording in Latin that it was he, Johannes Alexander Thynne, who had newly built and decorated this sumptuous room in 1875.

14 Hugh Lupus, 1st Duke of Westminster: one of the richest and most highly respected Victorian land-owners with 30,000 acres in Cheshire and an income of more than £250,000 a year from the Grosvenor estate in London. T. Barlow after Sir John Everett Millais R.A.

Fortunately the Marquess of Bath was too busy 'Italianizing' the interior of Longleat to tamper with the ravishingly beautiful park created by 'Capability' Brown in the previous century. But a desire to show off and 'to command attention' spread through the upper classes like an epidemic and many a country house of elegant Georgian proportions was done over in a more elaborate and ostentatious style or torn down and rebuilt altogether. Architects were willing to design whatever 'effects' their rich clients required, from neo-classical Greek and Roman to Gothic, Tudor, Jacobean and French Renaissance, and it did not much matter if the overall effect was impure, pompous and extravagant so long as it did 'command attention'.

Sir Charles Barry, the architect of the new Palace of Westminster, 'Jacobeanized' Highclere House for the Earl of Carnavon and 'Tudorized' Canford Manor for Lady Charlotte Guest and her rich husband. He enlarged Harewood House, obscuring Adam's original design, and remodelled the gardens with formal flower beds set in ugly parterres of coloured gravel, miles of balustrading and innumerable flights of steps leading from one ornamental terrace to the next. And even more colossal in scale was the work he did for the Duke of Sutherland not only at Trentham Hall in Staffordshire, but at Cliveden in Buckinghamshire, where, overlooking one of the most beautiful reaches of the Thames, he built a Renaissance palace of a size and grandeur fit for royalty, the house towering above a spectacular balustraded terrace crowned with 42 enormous classical urns.

15 Eaton Hall in Cheshire. The enormous Victorian Gothic pile with clock tower and chapel built by Alfred Waterhouse for the 1st Duke of Westminster in 1874 on the site of an earlier mansion

Cliveden was built in 1851. Twenty-five years later the immense Victorian Gothic pile of Eaton Hall in Cheshire was created by Alfred Waterhouse for the 1st Duke of Westminster at a cost of £603,000 6s 11d. The Duke, whose Grosvenor ancestors went back to the time of William the Conqueror, was described as 'a great Victorian gentleman, who, while following the same pursuits and amusements as other Englishmen of wealth and leisure, devoted a great part of his time to those less fortunate than himself.' He was a superb shot, Master of the Cheshire Hunt and the owner of a racing stable that produced five Derby winners. But he disapproved of gambling and never laid a bet in his life, and 'he could pass from the race course to a missionary meeting without incurring the censure of even the strictest.' Countless charitable institutions of which he was the revered chairman benefited from his sober judgment and his income of more than £250,000 a year from the Grosvenor estate in London.

Eaton Hall was an enormous building designed for the Duke's grandfather, the 1st Marquess of Westminster. Waterhouse, the architect of the new Town Hall in Manchester, made it bigger still. He added a private wing to which the Duke and Duchess retired when they were not entertaining, a chapel embellished with stained glass by a Manchester artist, Frederick Shields, a huge domestic wing, a stable block and new coach houses, the whole massive edifice with mullioned and transomed windows, soaring pinnacles, horizontal balustrading and verticle towers resembling, when he had finished with it, a cross between a German cathedral and a gloomy House of Correction.

Waterhouse maintained that his eclectic Gothic style was 'perfectly suited to modern needs', and the Duke and Duchess were delighted. They could boast of the biggest and most efficient country house in the neighbourhood with an indoor staff of 50 servants and a dining-room large enough to seat 60 house guests without overcrowding. Bathrooms, though few in number, were equally spacious, with a fireplace in them, 'a reclining bath' surrounded by mahogany panels and a somewhat complicated apparatus of taps and showers which did not always perform quite as they should, so that some guests preferred to bathe in their own rooms in the steaming hot water poured by the servants into a copper hip bath set in front of the fire.

Smoking was forbidden altogether at Eaton Hall, but elsewhere as one writer observed: 'The pitiable resources to which some gentlemen are driven, even in their own houses, in order to be able to enjoy the pestiferous luxury of a cigar, have now given rise to the occasional introduction of an apartment dedicated to the use of Tobacco.' If the Billiard Room was not available, 'a retreat for the smoker', suitably clad in a frogged smoking jacket and a velvet cap, could sometimes be provided 'where the *dolce far niente* of this particular enjoyment may solely and undisturbedly reign.'

A fairly strict code of behaviour had to be observed if country house life was to be organized smoothly for the comfort of the family and their numerous guests. Elaborate meals had to be on time if chaos was to be avoided in the kitchen and servants given their orders well in advance if their

16 The Great Drawing-Room at Eaton Hall, elaborately decorated in the Gothic style with a fan-vaulted ceiling inspired by the ecclesiastical fervour of mid-Victorian taste

duties were to be performed silently and efficiently. But most of the guests were already familiar with each other and if this sometimes led to an intolerable state of boredom, it also encouraged a feeling of upper-class solidarity as of one big family. Through intermarriage the leading aristocratic families were all related to one another, a whole network of exclusive family connections spreading outwards and downwards to the lesser nobility and the gentry. In consequence house parties and shooting parties were made up of the same people from one country house to the next with a fringe of social climbers who had been successful in breaking into the magic circle. These were the men of talent in literature and science, the up and coming Members of Parliament and the bankers and industrialists of the second and third generations, who made themselves acceptable by conforming to the standards of those with high birth and breeding.

Both Thackeray and Carlyle were entertained at the Grange in Hampshire by Lady Ashburton, a daughter of the Earl of Sandwich, who had married the immensely rich banker, William Baring, before he succeeded to his father's title of Lord Ashburton. Considered to be the cleverest and most brilliant hostess of the 1840s and 1850s, she was 'tall and commanding in appearance without any pretensions to good looks', very arrogant and overbearing, but 'endowed with intelligence, taste and wit'. Apparently her husband was quite content to stand in the background while she dominated the company she gathered round her and though her wit, like that of so many successful hostesses, could often be cruel and devastating, her victims always returned for more punishment. Mortally wounded by one of her crushing sarcasms, Thackeray once sent her a drawing of himself kneeling at her feet with his hair aflame from the hot coals she was pouring on his head out of an ornamental brazier. And Carlyle, though disapproving of fashionable Society, was irresistibly drawn towards her.

Indeed, Lady Harriet could do no wrong in the eyes of the rugged Scotch philosopher. If he sometimes envied Monckton Milnes for his easy adaptability to her capriciousness, he was none the less thoroughly at home in her house and her willing slave, much to the annoyance of his wife, Jane, who positively hated the Grange. 'The very look of the bedroom with its immense dimensions, its vaulted and carved ceiling, its princely magnificence of every sort, makes me feel ill at ease,' she wrote. 'I feel I have got out of my latitude — as much as if I were hanging on to the horns of the moon! — and then the recollection of all the idle restless people under the same roof with me — whose idleness and restlessness is so contagious! In fact *this* is "a country house" with a vengeance! and I do not find my Destiny has done amiss in casting *my* lot amongst "the poorer orders".'

Jane, knowing she had only been invited 'to keep up appearances as the wife of Mr C.', found her hostess condescending—'very *kind* to me after her fashion' — and went on to describe the Grange in her own vivid style. 'The Place itself is like, not *one*, but a conglomeration of Greek Temples set down in a magnificent wooded Park some five miles in length. The inside is magnificent to death — the ceilings all painted in fresco — some dozen public rooms on the ground floor all hung with magnificent paintings — and fitted up like an Arabian night's entertainment.' And what with 'the perpetual tumult of arriving and departing guests — in all *my* life I never drew breath in such a racket!' Jane felt she could not get back to her own modest home in Cheyne Row quickly enough.

Lord Ashburton, it was said, sacrificed what might have been a successful political career to the demands made on him by his domineering wife. Disraeli did the opposite. He married Mary Anne Wyndham, a middle-aged widow with money, as an ally towards the achievement of his great ambition. As a young man, familiar with Count d'Orsay and the somewhat disreputable Lady Blessington, he had shocked the House of Commons with his purple velvet trousers, yellow waistcoats and gold jewellery; but he quickly saw the need of becoming a respectable landowner with a respectable wife if his career in Parliament was to prosper, and in 1848, shortly before his marriage, he bought the manor of Hughenden in Buckinghamshire with money borrowed from Lord George Bentinck.

He was not at all interested in hunting or shooting and his too exaggerated country clothes never succeeded in disguising his enigmatic, oriental appearance. He took care, however, to perform all the conventional duties of a country squire with dignity, sitting on the bench as a Justice of the Peace, attending Quarter Sessions at Aylesbury and wooing the worthies of High Wycombe. He entertained the bishop and allowed his grounds to be used for village fêtes and garden parties, ably supported by Mary Anne, who adored him and was, in his view, in spite of the eccentric way she got herself up in pink satin with rivers of lace and diamond buttons, 'ever the perfect wife'.

Some of the long established county families found it difficult to accept an outsider like Disraeli and were even more shocked by the invasion of the shires by the *nouveaux riches* bankers and industrialists, whose wealth was often far in excess of their own. Yet money did begin to count as time went on and provided the newcomers behaved circumspectly and adapted themselves to the prevailing habits of the countryside, it was nobody's business to enquire how they had managed to achieve such opulence. Prosperity covered a multitude of sins, and Lord Shaftesbury, who persistently strove to limit the working hours of women and children, was considered a dangerous fanatic bent on the destruction of the *status quo* between the labouring classes and their masters; for to the self-made men of the new plutocracy, the industrial methods of the nineteenth century did not seem unjust and it was perfectly possible for them to worship God and Mammon at one and the same time without any feeling of inconsistency.

Their one great ambition was to be taken for country gentlemen and with this in mind, they did all the things that were expected of them. They built colossal houses, as big or bigger than, Woburn and Chatsworth. They endowed schools and alms-houses in the village and sent their wives and daughters out with jellies and broth and blankets to the sick and elderly on their estates. They kept horses and carriages and rode to hounds with their aristocratic neighbours, and although their wealth was not derived from the land and their roots were not there either, the sons of the gentry were not averse to marrying their daughters if a satisfactory dowry could be arranged.

Several members of the fabulous Rothschild family, grandsons of a *Judenstrasse* pedlar (the street in Frankfurt to which the Jews were confined) settled in Disraeli's beloved 'beechy Bucks', buying up land in the Vale of Aylesbury. There was Baron Lionel, who advanced the four million sterling Disraeli needed for his Suez Canal coup, with 3,500 acres at Tring and the seventeenth-century manor house which had once been the home of Nell Gwynn. Then there were Lionel's two brothers, Anthony at Aston Clinton and Meyer at Mentmore Towers, a luxurious Anglo-Norman castellated mansion designed for him by Joseph Paxton and surrounded by groves of trees, rich pastures, a stud farm and a racing stable. 'The Medicis were never lodged so in the height of their glory' was Lady Eastlake's somewhat acid comment on Mentmore, where the hunting, the shooting and the garden fêtes, the carriage drives and Lucullan picnics of lobster mousse, salmon soufflés and champagne, provided a continuous round of bucolic pleasure in the lush green beauty of the English countryside.

Meyer was popular with the local people. His enthusiasm for racing and breeding horses endeared him to everyone and his ostentatious display was combined with a marvellous generosity. No beggar was ever turned away from his gate and his farm labourers, grooms, servants and gamekeepers were highly paid and well cared for. When he died in 1874, he left Mentmore and a fortune of £2,000,000 in cash to his only daughter, Hannah, who was courted by the young Earl of Rosebery. As she was 27, rather stout and not a beauty, it was widely reported that Rosebery was after her money, which was quite untrue. 'I am very happy in my engagement,' he wrote to a friend. 'You do not know my future wife. She is very simple, very unspoilt, very clever, very warm-hearted and very shy.... I never knew such a beautiful character.'

They were married in 1878, Disraeli giving the bride away and 'acting the heavy father *à ravir*.' But the Rothschilds did not need this alliance with the aristocracy to establish their place in Society. Ferdinand, an Austrian cousin of Baron Lionel, and the Baron's three sons, Natty, Leo and Alfred, had

17 The pseudo-oriental Smoking Room of the Duke of Saxe-Coburg and Gotha at Clarence House, London, where the gentlemen retired to enjoy 'the pestiferous luxury of a cigar'

already become close friends of the Prince of Wales, who found their company gay and amusing and very useful when he ran out of funds, as he so often did. Rothschild money had the virtue of never running out — it flowed in a splendid river of liquid gold; and none of them ever grudged a penny spent on giving pleasure.

Ferdinand spent a fortune on Waddesdon Manor, a gigantic pile of stone copied from the chateaux of the Loire and featuring the towers of Maintenon, the chimneys of Chambord and the staircases of Blois in the midst of rural Buckinghamshire. He had the top of a hill sliced off and levelled down to sustain his colossal mansion, transplanted thousands of large forest trees and shrubs to the vicinity, bought fountains, peacocks and statuary to adorn his terraced walks and built glasshouses of a mile or more in extent to provide him with peaches, nectarines, muscat grapes, arum lilies and orchids at all seasons of the year. Indoors there were 222 rooms sumptuously decorated with ornate panelling, painted ceilings, marble floors and carved chimney-pieces, with Louis Quinze and Louis Seize gilt furniture, Sèvres china, Savonnerie carpets, embroidered curtains, Beauvais tapestries and *objets*

18 A house-party in 1891 at Easton Lodge, the home of Lord and Lady Brooke. *From left to right (standing)* Lord Algernon Lennox, Count Mensdorff, Lady Eva Greville, the Prince of Wales, Lady Brooke, Princess Victoria Mary of Teck, the Duchess of Teck; *(seated)* Prince Francis of Teck, Lady Kaye, Lord Brooke, Lady Lilian Wemyss, the Marquis de Soveral

d'art of every conceivable sort and size from the smallest Fabergé Easter egg to an outsize musical elephant with jewelled eyes.

As a host, Ferdinand left nothing to chance. His guests were awakened by footmen in powdered wigs, followed by an underling pushing a breakfast trolley and were invited to choose 'tea or coffee or a peach off the wall'; and if they chose tea, were asked if they preferred China, Indian or Ceylon, with lemon, milk or cream; and if with milk, 'Jersey, Hereford or Shorthorn'. At luncheon the same bewildering variety was offered and at dinner the chef created one dish after another of exquisite flavour and superb aesthetic appearance. Ferdinand, by a wave of his hand, seemed able to satisfy the most hedonistic taste in the world, and when the visitors went away, their broughams were piled high with hot-house fruit and flowers to take home.

The Prince of Wales frequently stayed at Waddesdon surrounded by fashionable Society, or what the widowed Queen called 'the fast racing set!', the people of whom she had always disapproved, the people she now believed were leading her son down the awful road to ruin. Why did he not choose his friends with more discretion? Why was he not more like his dear Papa? Why

19 In the Entrance Hall at Sandringham House, the country home of the Prince and Princess of Wales, visitors placed their cards on a silver tray held in the outstretched paws of a stuffed bear

20 After luncheon in the Great Hall at Sandringham, where the parrot squawked in its cage and the antlered heads of many a noble stag gazed down on the royal house-party

indeed? Shut in the gloom of Windsor Castle and Osborne, perpetually mourning her lost lord and master, it never occurred to her that the frustrated Prince needed more and more social diversion to offset his mother's obstinate refusal to allow him any active role in the affairs of state, which, so she said, she alone could handle. 'It is *quite clear,* the Prince of Wales has *no right to meddle,'* she told Lord Hartington, and when Gladstone suggested some responsible work should be found for him, she was even more offended. The heavy burden she had to carry wore her out and made her feel quite ill, but she did not trust her son, she never had — and he knew it.

She never stopped nagging him about the company he and the Princess of Wales kept. There was so much vice among the aristocracy, it was their duty, she told them, 'to deny themselves amusement' in order to keep up 'that tone which used to be the Pride of England.' They must show their disapproval of the idleness and frivolity of high Society 'by *not* asking people like the Duchess of Manchester to dinner or down to Sandringham and above all by *not* going to their houses.' 'Many with whom I have conversed,' the Queen went on anxiously, 'tell me that at no time for the last sixty or seventy years was frivolity, the love of pleasure, self-indulgence, and idleness (producing ignorance) carried to such excess as now in the Higher Classes, and that it resembles the time before the French Revolution; and I must — alas! — admit that this *is true*. Believe me! It is *most alarming,* although you do not observe it, nor will you *hear* it; but those who do not live *in* the gay circle of fashion, and who view it calmly, are greatly, seriously ALARMED.' To this agitated letter, the Prince replied gravely and politely, and then continued his round of country house visits as before.

He was not an easy guest. No one could be more charming, more affable, or more kind and considerate; but anyone who mistook his tolerance for familiarity and showed him the least disrespect was liable to be snubbed very firmly. Gentlemen, smoking, laughing or drinking with him and playing baccarat or whist until long after midnight, knew exactly how far they could go, enduring his silly practical jokes and his occasional outbursts of rage with stoicism. Ladies, watching his hooded, blue-grey eyes, were quickly aware of whether he was bored or not, and when he travelled around with Princess Alexandra, they kept their distance. When he travelled *en garçon,* things were different. His hostess saw to it that he was comfortable and his bedroom not too far away from that of the lady in whom he was for the moment most interested.

Provided there was no hint of scandal and the unwritten rules of conduct were observed, country house parties from Saturday to Monday (it was vulgar to talk of week-ends) gave the guests marvellous opportunities to indulge in their illicit love affairs. A plate of sandwiches left outside the door of a lady's bedroom had a significance that was understood by everyone — except the German diplomat, Baron von Eckardstein, who was wandering down a corridor at Chatsworth one night and feeling hungry, proceeded to make a meal of them, much to the dismay of the amorous countess who had put them there as a pre-arranged signal to her lover. Other indications – picking up the silver candlestick before going up to bed with a particular gesture and a winning glance – served the same purpose; and at Easton Lodge, the home of 'Daisy' Brooke (later Countess of Warwick), the hostess was always careful to remind her guests that the stable bell rang at 6 o'clock in the morning. At that hour the corridors were empty, and any gentleman who failed to heed the bell as a warning to return quickly to his own bedroom, was a fool. At breakfast three hours later, both he and the lady whose favour he had enjoyed, came into the dining-room without betraying anything more than a polite interest in the weather, and though everyone knew what was going on, nothing was said.

These clandestine arrangements suited His Royal Highness very well and were accepted by his wife with a good grace. In their own country home at Sandringham, which Princess Alexandra loved very dearly, there was an atmosphere of gaiety and fun, with children running about all over the house and dogs everywhere, and a large, stuffed bear standing in the hall with a silver plate for visitor's cards in its outstretched paws. Converted at a cost of some £300,000 from a simple Georgian country villa into a large mock-Tudor mansion, the house was a typical product of the mid-Victorian ideal of excessive ornamentation. Inside it was crammed with fussy, suffocating furniture: chairs and sofas covered in chintz, pleated lampshades with bows on them, whatnots supporting countless ornaments and souvenirs, and small tables with tortured legs, each bearing its load of family photographs in silver and velvet frames, and all reflecting a deplorable lack of taste.

Lady Macclesfield wondered why, with the whole of England to choose from, the Prince should have settled on Sandringham with its bleak and ugly surroundings, 'no fine trees, no water, no hills', only fields of turnips and the east wind blowing in from the North Sea. But the Prince and his wife were happy there. He enjoyed living like a country squire and was interested in his farms and piggeries. On Sundays he took his guests to church in the morning and when luncheon was over, led them round the estate to admire the stables and the kitchen garden, several dogs following at his heels and his pockets full of sugar lumps for the horses. Then after this informal tour was over, the ladies changed into elaborate and flimsy tea-gowns and everyone assembled in the hall for 5 o'clock tea, dispersing an hour or so later to change again into full evening dress for dinner. The Prince arranged the seating at the table himself and an equerry stood by to explain to each gentleman who was to be his partner and where he was to sit.

Weekdays were dedicated to shooting. The sandy soil of Sandringham was particularly suited to the rearing of pheasants and partridges and the royal gamekeepers wearing green velvet coats and bowler hats trimmed with a gold cord, were well instructed and efficient. The *battue* system, which the Prince Consort had favoured, was now generally adopted, with a horde of beaters in smocks and black felt hats decorated with blue and red ribbons, remorselessly driving the birds towards the guns. A sudden and terrible fusillade rattled the bright air with birds dropping out of the sky in all

21 H.R.H. the Prince of Wales with a shooting party at Sandringham, where the soil was particularly suited to the rearing of pheasants and partridges and the Prince enjoyed the life of a country squire

directions or wheeling about in anguished confusion; then the shooters retired to the next fence with their camp stools and their cigars until another flock of birds could be driven towards them.

Luncheon was brought down from the house and served in a large tent, where the gentlemen were joined by the ladies and everyone had to listen while the Prince read out the morning's score, pausing for applause when a gun was credited with a good bag. The tent was very cold because the Prince always insisted on the flaps being folded up, and some of the ladies were not over enthusiastic about watching the shoot in the afternoon, as this meant sitting behind a hedge in the disagreeable wind and waiting for the next holocaust. But even Queen Victoria did not complain of the time and money her son devoted to shooting. It was a manly occupation and one which his 'dear Papa' had enjoyed. The game larder at Sandringham was a big one. It had to be when the day's bag often ran to 3000 birds, 6000 hares and rabbits and a number of other feathered and furred creatures.

3

The London Season

Of all the rituals observed by the Victorian upper classes, the London Season was the most important. It coincided with the parliamentary session from Easter to August, which brought the country gentlemen to town, and gave their ladies a glorious opportunity to show themselves off, to find husbands for their daughters and to enjoy a round of Metropolitan gaiety and pleasure not to be had in the shires.

London to all appearances was the most opulent city in the world. Still graced by the elegant architecture of the eighteenth century and the splendid 'improvements' of John Nash and the Prince Regent, the West End had an air of distinction. The leafy squares, Hyde Park, the spacious crescents in Belgravia and the streets of Mayfair and St James's were filled with spick and span carriages, a smart equipage with coachman and footman being an absolute necessity for anyone wishing to cut a figure in Society. Even Thackeray impulsively bought a hackney cab and its driver one day and dolled them up to take him from Kensington to the great world of Park Lane and Piccadilly.

For the gracious inhabitants of this great world, the poverty of the East End and the grey areas of middle-class respectability in between, did not exist. Only a few eccentrics, like the young Baroness Burdett-Coutts and Lord Shaftesbury, were aware of the chronic, insanitary overcrowding in Clerkenwell and Bethnal Green, of the sickness, crime and destitution in Soho and Seven Dials out of sight behind the grand façade of Regent Street. Ladies descending from their carriages to enter Farmer & Roger's Great Cloak & Shawl Emporium in this most fashionable of shopping streets, never came into contact with the population on the east side of it; and if they sometimes complained of the pasty-faced shop-assistants being tired and dispirited, it was because they knew nothing of the battle to survive the more genteel poverty of the suburbs, nothing of standing on their feet all day at the beck and call of a cantankerous shop-walker or of being pleasant to the many capricious customers who taxed their patience to the limit.

Yet the ladies of Victorian upper-class Society were not without charity or a sense of responsibility. It was simply that they believed 'Providence had ordained the different orders and gradations into which the human family is divided', that some people were born to a high and privileged position of wealth and security and some not. In the country, where everyone knew everyone else and the tenants depended on the protection of their lord and master, there was no ill-feeling between the rich and the poor and plenty of room for personal benevolence. In the ever-growing, overcrowded Metropolis, things were different. The London mob could be positively dangerous when stirred up by the Radical politicians and the less one had to do with it the better; though, of course, it was amusing when the riff-raff from nowhere gathered round the awning in the square on a ball night to watch the handsome and bejewelled guests arriving. They really seemed to enjoy themselves, laughing and whistling and sometimes making rude Cockney jokes about the fashionable 'swells'. It was only Florence Nightingale, as a young girl in Society, who noticed their drawn faces and ragged garments, carrying the image of them with her into the dazzling ball-room.

The nobility owned town houses as superb as their country seats. Devonshire House on Piccadilly, overlooking Green Park, had a magnificent ball-room, where the bachelor Duke and the Burlington cousin who succeeded him in 1858, entertained in the tradition set by their extravagant forbears. Bath House to the west of Devonshire House was the home of Lady Ashburton, and the nearby Cambridge House of Lord and Lady Palmerston, whose receptions were an outstanding feature of every Season from 1855 to 1865 when Palmerston, as Prime Minister, was ruling the country with great vigour and self-confidence. Both of them were no longer young and it was

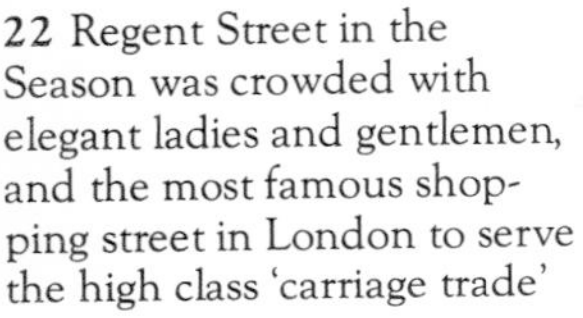

22 Regent Street in the Season was crowded with elegant ladies and gentlemen, and the most famous shopping street in London to serve the high class 'carriage trade'

said by one malicious person that when Emily forgot her rouge and Palmerston omitted to dye his whiskers, a real crisis in the affairs of the nation could be inferred. Yet no one ever refused an invitation to Cambridge House and many a political reputation was made, or unmade, under the glittering chandelier in the Grand Saloon.

Lansdowne House, round the corner in Berkeley Square, built by Adam in 1765, was the home of the 3rd Marquess of Landsdowne, a leading figure in the Whig heirarchy. According to the mischief-making Princess Lieven, he was 'the most distinguished of all the great aristocrats of this country [England] without a spot on his reputation' and as her nose for scandal was highly sensitive, he must indeed have been a paragon. He had a picture gallery at Lansdowne House and a large sculpture gallery filled with Greek and Roman marbles, and was a patron of contemporary art and letters, welcoming Macaulay, Thackeray, Ruskin and Millais among others to his dinner table.

Thackeray enjoyed himself immensely at Lansdowne House. After the success of *Vanity Fair* he was asked everywhere. 'All of a sudden I am a great man,' he told his mother. 'I am ashamed of it, but yet I can't help seeing it – being elated by it and trying to keep it down'; and although Macaulay suspected that success had gone to his head, in reality the lavish hospitality of his new friends amused the author of *Vanity Fair* as much as it gratified him. 'I reel from dinner party to dinner party – I wallow in turtle and swim in Shampang!' he wrote, while admitting that he took the utmost delight in 'luxurious and well-lighted rooms, good music, excellent wines and cookery, exhilarating talk, gay and airy gossip, pretty women and their *toilettes* and refined and noble manners.'

Not everyone enjoyed going into Society as much as that. Jane Carlyle was persuaded by her husband to attend a ball at Bath House in 1850. At first she refused for the want of a dress and the horror of *'stripping'* herself, after being 'muffled up' for so many years against the cold and the damp of Chelsea. But Carlyle bullied her into accepting, so she ordered a white silk dress, which 'first was made high and long sleeved and then on the very day of the ball,' as she told her cousin, Helen Welsh, 'was sent back to be cut down to the due pitch of indecency! I could have gone into *fits* of crying when I began to put it on,' she wrote, 'but I looked so astonishingly well in it by *candlelight* and when I got into the fine rooms amongst the universally *bare* people I felt so much in *keeping*, that I forgot my neck and arms almost immediately. I was glad *after* that I went – not for any pleasure I had at the time being past dancing and knowing but few people – but it is an additional idea of life to have seen such a party – all the Duchesses one ever heard tell of blazing in diamonds, all the young beauties of the Season, all the distinguished statesmen, etc. etc. were to be seen among the six or seven hundred people present – and the room hung with artificial roses looked like an Arabian Nights entertainment.' What pleased Jane most was the good look she got *'into the eyes'* of the old Duke of Wellington: 'one has no notion seeing him in the streets what a dear kind face he has,' she declared; and then she added with more than a touch of asperity: 'Lady Ashburton receiving all these people with her grand-lady airs was also a sight worth seeing.'

Poor Jane! She could not – and never did – quite forgive Mr C. for his devotion to his goddess. 'That eternal Bath House,' she wrote later in her diary. 'I wonder how many thousand miles Mr C. has walked between there and here [Cheyne Row] putting it all together; setting up always another milestone betwixt himself and me. Oh, good gracious! when I first noticed that heavy yellow house without knowing, or caring to know, who it belonged to, how far was I from dreaming that through years and years I should carry every stone's weight of it on my heart.' Only the death of Lady Ashburton in 1857, which left Mr C. looking 'like a child who has lost his nurse in a wood', freed Jane from the jealous fury she harboured against this accomplished but condescending lady, who so often pampered her male guests at the expense of their wives.

What Jane failed to realize was that entertaining for the Season on the grand scale required a certain ruthless determination from the hostesses, who vied with each other to make their receptions a success. Royal favour was eagerly sought, though Queen Victoria and Prince Albert only honoured the most respectable houses with their presence and the guests invited to meet them all belonged to the most exclusive families. In June 1849 they attended a banquet and a ball given by the Duke and Duchess of Norfolk at Norfolk House in St James's Square and the Queen danced every number, except the polka, leaving with her husband at five minutes past

23 The splendid banquet given by the Duke and Duchess of Norfolk at Norfolk House, St James's Square for H.M. the Queen and Prince Albert in the summer of 1849. The banquet was followed by a grand ball

midnight. A few nights later the royal couple visited the 2nd Marquess of Westminster (father of the 1st Duke) at Grosvenor House, his palatial mansion on Park Lane, built by Cundy in 1842, with a handsome Corinthian colonnade based on Trajan's Roman Forum, a superb picture gallery and a magnificent dining-room, which for this occasion was resplendent with an array of gold plate such as even the Queen herself could not surpass. She sat between the Marquess and the Archbishop of Canterbury, and the other guests included the Queen of the Belgians, the Duke and Duchess of Norfolk, Earl Spencer, the Marquess of Lansdowne and several members of the Grosvenor family.

After the banquet more guests arrived for a concert in the picture gallery, featuring Signor Costa of the Royal Italian Opera House, Covent Garden,

24 The magnificent Picture Gallery at Grosvenor House, Park Lane, where the Queen and Prince Albert were entertained in 1849 by the 2nd Marquess of Westminster (father of the 1st Duke). The leading singers from the Royal Opera House gave a concert of Italian music

and the famous singers Mario, Tamburini and Lablache with Madame Persiani and Mademoiselle de Meric. They sang excerpts from Donizetti's *Lucia di Lammermoor*, Rossini's *Tancredi*, Cimarosa's *Matrimonio Segreto* and Mozart's *Nozze di Figaro*; and in the interval, 'the windows at the rear of the mansion were opened to discover a brilliant illumination in the gardens, the green sward and branches of the trees being thickly studded with variegated lamps.' The picture gallery was also 'superbly illuminated' to show off the colossal Rubens of *The Israelites Gathering Manna*, the Titians, the Claudes and the Rembrandts, Gainsborough's *Blue Boy* and Reynold's *Mrs Siddons as the Tragic Muse*. With all this – the music, the paintings, the gold plate and the distinction of the assembled company – Mademoiselle de Schimmelpenninck, daughter of His Excellency the Minister for the Netherlands, was quite overcome by the splendour of the English aristocracy, while the noble Marquess and his lady, who on less royal occasions had a reputation for being notoriously stingy, could congratulate themselves on the brilliance of their expensive entertainment.

The singers could also congratulate themselves on the enormous fees they

25 The fashionable audience leaving the Royal Opera House, Covent Garden, after a performance in 1842. Carriages drove up to the door under the portico, which sheltered the ladies in unseasonable weather. Eugene Lami

26 H.M. the Queen and Prince Albert in the Royal Box at the Italian Opera House in the Haymarket. It was not etiquette for the Mistress of the Robes and other members of the royal entourage to be seated; they remained standing through the entire performance

were able to earn in a single evening, for nowhere in the world were they paid so much as in London in the 1840s and 1850s and nowhere acclaimed with more enthusiasm. Italian opera had always been popular with the aristocratic *cognoscenti* and it was the fashionable thing to do to take a subscription for the Season and to invite one's friends to come along. But as the lights in the auditorium did not go down during the performance, many of the boxholders were far more interested in showing themselves off and gossiping with their acquaintances than in the action on the stage, only interrupting their chatter occasionally to listen to a favourite aria sung by the leading prima donna. None the less a very high standard of singing was demanded and between 1847 and 1852, two Italian opera seasons ran side by side with Jenny Lind and Henriette Sontag at Her Majesty's Theatre in the Haymarket, and Grisi, Persiani, Alboni, Mario, Tamburini and Pauline Viardot at the Royal Italian Opera House, Covent Garden. Not only the well-known works of Rossini, Donizetti and Bellini were performed, but those of the young Italian composer, Guiseppe Verdi, and of Gounod and Meyerbeer, whose opera *Les Hugenots* was given in Italian as *Gli Ugonotti*.

Queen Victoria as a girl had studied singing with Lablache and Prince Albert was something of a composer as well as an organist. Their more serious approach to music had a profound effect on the behaviour of the audiences at the Royal Italian Opera House and their musical parties at

Buckingham Palace were big events of the Season. Jenny Lind, with a voice of incomparable beauty and enhanced by a reputation for the blameless purity of her private life, was the Queen's favourite singer and the young and handsome Mendelssohn her favourite composer. When Prince Albert invited him to play the organ at Buckingham Palace one afternoon, the Queen sang some of his songs with a simplicity and a natural sweetness of tone that pleased the young German immensely; and later, after the successful first performance of his new oratorio, *Elijah*, the royal couple persuaded him to play at one of their musical evenings.

But the biggest and most important events of the Season at Buckingham Palace were the four Drawing-Rooms held by the Queen for the presentation of the débutantes, the young daughters of the nobility and the gentry entering, or rather 'coming out' in Society for the first time. These afternoon parties, at which everyone wore full evening dress, had been moved from the cramped State Apartments at St James's Palace to the new Throne Room at Buckingham Palace and were strictly controlled by the Lord Chamberlain and his officers. Only the wives and daughters of the aristocracy, the country and town gentry and the higher ranks of the Church, the armed forces and the legal profession, with a selected few of the new bankers and industrialists, were given the entrée and permitted to attend. Even then their birth, wealth

27 The Royal Drawing-Room in the Throne Room at Buckingham Palace in 1861. Presentation at Court was the most important event of the Season for the wives and daughters of the nobility and gentry

and associations were very carefully scrutinized before the privilege of being presented to the Sovereign was granted, on the assumption that anyone involved, or likely to be involved, in a scandal of any sort was not a fit person to be received at Court. Only married ladies of impeccable virtue, in theory if not in practice, were allowed to present their daughters or someone else's daughter who had married into the family, though a good deal of manoeuvring around this restriction enabled the high-ranking dowagers to extend their patronage beyond their immediate circle, especially in the later years of the Queen's reign when Society became less exclusive.

The actual moment of presentation to the Queen passed very quickly, but the preparations for the ceremony were formidable and very expensive. Not only did the young ladies have to learn how to curtsy and to retire backwards out of the royal presence without tripping over a train of some three and a half or four yards in length, but they had to submit to a Court hairdresser, hoping he would arrange their coiffeur so that it would support without mishap the three white plumes and the veil they had to wear. Visits to the Court dressmaker were prolonged and sometimes exasperating. Plump girls, not long out of the schoolroom, had to be stuffed into hideously tight corsets to achieve the necessary small waist and plain girls with long necks were thrust into demure dresses with the corsage cut low to accentuate the drooping line of the shoulders.

Not every girl was blessed with natural elegance and charm, or, as the reporter of the *Illustrated London News* gushingly suggested, 'longing to take her first bound into the delirious circle of pleasure from the footstool of the throne, and to wear her first trousseau at the Court among the fairest aristocrats, sunning their peerless pride in the smiles of royalty.' Some of them were shy and awkward, their complexions – as God made them and without the help of cosmetics – suffering from the heat or the cold and the strain on their nerves. Some found sitting in the long queue of family coaches waiting in the Mall with the populace staring in at the windows, an ordeal – it was not the thing to do to pull the blinds down and thereby deny the *hoi polloi* their amusement. Then when the Palace was reached at last, there was another long and exhausting wait before the anxious moment arrived of being ushered into the Throne Room.

It was – again in the words of the fulsome reporter of the *Illustrated London News* – 'the accomplished Peeress, who is farther into life's summer and wears the rose of beauty in its fullest blowing and its deepest blush ... with her lofty bearing and her fine haughty self-possession', who apparently shone most brightly at the Drawing-Room, 'secure in the noblest realization of aristocratic pride.' The *grandes dames* of the Court certainly vied with each other in the splendour of their *toilettes* and the display of their family jewels. The Duchess of Argyll wore 'a train of blue velvet lined with satin and trimmed with bouquets of green and brown oak leaves, a petticoat of blue satin flowered with guipure lace, and a tiara of diamonds and oak leaves, with feathers and lace lappets.' The Duchess of Norfolk had 'a train of white Gothic moiré, lined with glacé and trimmed with Irish point lace, a petticoat of white glacé flounced with Irish point, and a head-dress composed of feathers and lace lappets, ornamented with emeralds and diamonds.' And the Countess of Jersey appeared in 'a splendid Court costume composed of a white satin dress over two Oriental *tuniques,* embroidered and fringed with gold, a train of *drap d'or* trimmed with gold ribbon, a tiara and a stomacher of diamonds.'

The Countess no doubt felt it was necessary to put in a very grand appearance at Court to show that she had recovered from what the Duke of Wellington described as 'a horrible event in the Jersey family' – the elopement of her 17-year-old daughter Lady Adela with a Captain Ibbetson of the 11th Hussars, who carried her off to Gretna Green and then across the Channel to escape the family wrath. No one knew how Lady Adela had become acquainted with this 'whiskered gentleman', though enquiry among the servants revealed that she was in the habit of walking in the Park with her maid and had been frequently 'accosted' by him, and that the gallant Captain, who lived in a house not far from the Jerseys', had been seen constantly looking through a spy-glass directed towards the window of Lady Adela's room, besides making signals from his verandah. It was all quite dreadful and showed how dangerous it was for young ladies to go walking in the Park even with a maid. Lady Jersey had hysterics and the Earl was in a rage; but in the end all was forgiven and the young couple were rejoined in matrimony with the blessings of the Church.

As a marriage market the Season was notorious. Ambitious mothers put their daughters up for auction. In theory the girls had freedom of choice, but in practice pressure was brought to bear on them in several different ways and only the most headstrong among them dared to fall in love against the wishes of their parents or to encourage any young man without the necessary qualifications of birth, breeding and a good income. A great deal depended on the débutante's first ball and the impression she made there. If she was pretty and popular and everything went well, she was launched into the main stream of Society and surrounded by eager suitors. If she was not, she suffered the horrors of becoming a wallflower, of sitting out among the rows of chaperons nodding drowsily over their fans or examining the company disagreeably through their lorgnettes.

Caroline Lyttelton was big and clumsy and had been brought up in the country. Her first ball was at Devonshire House, where, according to her mother: 'She went with the highest expectation of pleasure and comfort, and found herself crowded, heated and frightened to death, asked to dance *instantly* by too kind a cousin, dragged into the first quadrille of 32 she had ever seen, and of course, got quizzed and pitied and does not wish to dance again.' She fell in love with a young man who sat next to her at a dinner party and fixed his eyes on her with what she believed to be 'his whole heart and soul'. His connections were good, he was a nephew of Lord Monteagle's, and he told her that she had 'a very enthusiastic temperament'; but shortly afterwards he married someone else and poor Caroline remained a spinster all her life.

Eligible young men were not always very keen to commit themselves and trying to catch them was by no means easy. Eldest sons, who would inherit a title or a fortune, or both, became the prey of the mothers with the highest aspirations for their daughters and assumed an importance quite beyond their individual merits. Not, however, for Lady Stanley of Alderley, who thought Lord Pomfret and Lord Goodrich 'two of the most insignificant, ugly little mortals' she had ever seen and who observed to her mother-in-law that 'eldest sons do not shine this year'. Both ladies were extremely agitated about the fate of Blanche Stanley, 'a dangerously romantic girl' in their opinion, much in need of guidance. 'You will be a lucky mother if you do keep clear of all shoals,' the Dowager Lady Stanley wrote to her daughter-in-law. 'The mischief is indeed soon done and it is difficult to push off the breakers in

28 The débutante's first ball was a test of her future popularity. If she was admired, her chances of finding a husband improved immeasurably

time, but the greatest difficulty is for the eyes of the parents to be sufficiently open.' Fortunately Blanche was manoeuvred away from the 'romantick dream of love at first sight' into the arms of her most persistent but painfully shy suitor, the young Earl of Airlie, who followed her to Alderley when the London Season was over. After a long and very cold walk in the woods when Airlie was so nervous he could not utter a word, he at last took the young lady's hand and did speak. She was 'thankful' he did not venture to kiss her, 'or to call her Blanche — all of which', as her mother sensibly suggested, 'she will get used to'.

Daughters depended a great deal on their mothers in choosing a husband; sons came up against the wrath of their fathers if they dared to select a bride thought to be unworthy of the family. At the age of 25, Lord Robert Cecil, heir to the 2nd Marquess of Salisbury, fell in love with Georgina Alderson, the eldest daughter of a distinguished East Anglian judge and a leading figure in the Church. Salisbury was furious. For one thing Miss Alderson had no fortune and for another her father belonged to the professional classes, a world the Marquess knew nothing about and did not wish to become involved with. His son, he thought, would make himself ridiculous by marrying beneath him and this misalliance would damage his future prospects in the Tory Party. As his elder brother, Lord Cranborne, was blind and crippled and unlikely to live very long, it was Lord Robert's duty to marry a woman of high birth, not to water the Cecil blood down with a non-entity unfit to rule as the mistress of Hatfield.

Lord Robert, however, was adamant. He reacted to his father's displeasure with dignity and great determination. He despised fashionable Society and disliked the 'empty-headed' daughters of the aristocracy paraded around the London Season by their worldly mothers. 'Miss Alderson suits me perfectly,' he wrote and while he was willing to accept Lord Salisbury's condition of a six months' separation to test his resolution, he went on to say: 'As I never remember to have receded from a resolution once deliberately taken, I do not anticipate much result from the present trial,' adding: 'I am exceedingly sorry that my adherence to this marriage should cause you annoyance; but my conviction that it is right is too strong to give it up, and it is my happiness, not yours that is at stake.' His conviction was entirely correct. Miss Alderson did suit him. Her strong and vigorous personality, her lively intelligence and her devotion not only gave him great happiness, but inspired him to go forward in his political career towards the ultimate achievement thrust upon him in 1885, when, as 3rd Marquess of Salisbury, he became Queen Victoria's most trusted Prime Minister.

The Duke and Duchess of Marlborough were thrown into a still worse state of disarray in 1872, when their second and favourite son, Lord Randolph Churchill, suddenly announced his intention of marrying Miss Jennie Jerome after four days' acquaintance with her at the Cowes Regatta. With lustrous dark hair, dazzling eyes and a figure that drew the attention of everyone when she walked into a room, she was the most beautiful of the three lovely daughters of an American businessman. Launched into Parisian

29 Jennie Jerome, the brilliant and beautiful daughter of an American businessman, who married Lord Randolph Churchill after a great deal of opposition from his aristocratic parents, the Duke and Duchess of Marlborough

Society by her ambitious mother, she was already a sophisticated young woman when they arrived in London after the Franco-Prussian War, and soon attracted a train of followers, excited by the uninhibited vitality she inherited from her father, her capacity for enjoying herself and her personal magnetism. Lord Randolph, when he saw her at a ball on board H.M.S. *Ariadne* given in honour of the Prince and Princess of Wales and the Tsar of Russia, was bewitched. The next day he met her 'by accident' when she was out walking and in the evening, after dinner at Mrs Jerome's rented house in Cowes, he proposed and was accepted.

Mrs Jerome, having set her sights rather higher than the second son of a Duke, was somewhat displeased. But her displeasure was nothing to the furore at Blenheim. The Duke and Duchess were disappointed in their irreligious, immoral eldest son, Blandford, and had pinned their hopes on his younger brother – and now here was Randolph asking their permission to marry an American of all things, and so infatuated with her, he had gone right out of his mind! 'You must imagine to yourself what must be our feelings at the prospect of this marriage of yours,' the Duke wrote. 'You cannot regard yourself alone in the matter and disassociate yourself from the rest of your family.... Under any circumstances, an American connection is not one that we would like.... You must allow it is a slightly coming down in pride for us to contemplate the connection.' And there was not even the saving grace of a fortune in the offing, for the Duke had made secret enquiries in New

30 Grosvenor Gate, Hyde Park in 1842, when bonnets and shawls and a prim, sentimental style of fashion appealed to the ladies in Society. T. Shotter Boys

York and did not like what he was told. 'Mr Jerome seems to be a sporting and I should think a vulgar kind of man,' he went on. 'I hear he drives about six and eight horses in New York (one may take this as a kind of indication of what the man is).' Moreover his finances seemed to be in a parlous state for the time being, owing to a fall in the Stock Market and his devotion to gambling.

Altogether the situation could not have been more unpromising. Both sides were obstinate. Jennie went back to Paris with her mother. Randolph, to please his father, agreed to stand as Tory candidate for the family borough of Woodstock and had a great victory over his Liberal opponent, and this at last induced the Marlboroughs to acquiesce rather grudgingly to his plans for the future. After protracted negotiations between the Duke's solicitor and Leonard Jerome, a financial settlement was finally agreed and the wedding

took place in Paris in 1874. The Duke and Duchess did not attend the ceremony: the Duchess said she was unwell.

By this time Society had changed greatly and the London Season had become more hectic, more extravagant and more cosmopolitan. For after the death of the Prince Consort and the retirement of the Queen into perpetual mourning, the pleasure-loving Prince of Wales had become the undisputed leader of fashion and the people round him, 'the Marlborough House Set', followed a new and more frivolous pattern of behaviour. Nothing reflected their attitude more vividly than the attire of the ladies. The prim, sentimental style of the 1840s and 50s with its drooping shoulder line and broad horizontal draping of the bust, was quite dead. So was the crinoline of the 60s, which had concealed the legs entirely under its voluminous dome of ruched satin, falling to the ground to cover the ankles and only showing the wearer's dainty little feet as she descended from her carriage. By 1866 the fashion was on the way out and Mrs Addley Bourne of Piccadilly, Family Draper, Jupon and Corset Manufacturer to the Court and Royal Family, only too anxious to get rid of her stock by advertising 'A THOUSAND CRINOLINES AT HALF PRICE commencing at 5s 11d, usually 10s 6d. Piccadilly Puffed Jupons 15s 6d; striped Linsey 8s 3d. Beautiful shapes, but a little dusty.' And by 1870 there was not a crinoline to be seen. The 'cuirasse bodice', moulded tightly to the bust and the smallest of small waists, had arrived, with the provocative bustle bunched up behind a narrow fronted skirt that accentuated the line of the hips. The bustle was decorated with elaborate bouffant trimmings and created by wearing a monstrous pad of horsehair tied to the waist with a tape over a corset made of whalebone and laced so tightly the wearer could hardly breathe.

Yet the fashion houses and the ladies themselves went mad to achieve this new look. It revealed the shapeliness of the female figure and demonstrated the new role of women in high Society, not simply as wives and mothers, but as glamorous beauties offering the male sex infinite opportunity for pleasure. At Ascot, Henley and Goodwood, at the receptions of the Season, familiarly known as Kettledrums or 'drums', at the Opera or strolling in Hyde Park at the fashionable hour of 5 o'clock, they showed off their charms and their willingness to gratify the immaculate gentlemen of their acquaintance. For while the widowed Queen continued to deplore the behaviour of 'the frivolous, selfish and pleasure-seeking rich', her son could not have too much of them and Marlborough House was a happy hunting ground for beautiful women, opulent financiers and the 'fast' members of the aristocracy. As he explained to his mother, the Prince felt he had 'certain duties to perform in London' which were all the more necessary because of her continued seclusion from public life. That he enjoyed these social duties, especially in the company of beautiful women, was quite beside the point. The Season was good for trade and good for London as the capital of a great and prosperous nation.

Hyde Park was the open air rendezvous of smart Society. In the early morning the gentlemen and a few of the more energetic ladies rode up and down the Row for exercise, with a sprinkling of 'pretty horsebreakers', young women of dubious origin, hoping to attract attention by their impudent good looks with every possibility of gaining a rich admirer and a toe-hold in Society. At noon, having changed from a riding habit into a smart costume, the ladies reappeared driving their own high-stepping horses in a phaeton or a tim-whisky with a diminutive groom sitting in the tiger seat. The Countess of Warwick remembered 'being surrounded by admiring friends when one pulled up at the entrance to the Row and chatted of the social round – of future meetings, of dances, lunches and dinners within "the Circle"', and added that her horses were so well known 'they always made a stir.' Later in the day, at 5 o'clock, it was not etiquette to handle the reins oneself, so the Park was filled with state carriages and open barouches driven by cockaded coachmen with one, or even two, footmen sitting up behind and the ladies within shading their delicate complexions with a variety of exquisite parasols. The middle classes of Bayswater and the *hoi polloi* from Pimlico stayed away from this opulent parade of fashion, but the little green chairs beside the Row and the South Drive were crowded with ladies and gentlemen who belonged – or hoped to belong – to Lady Warwick's exclusive circle; and when Lillie Langtry appeared in her smart carriage, the curiosity to see this celebrated beauty was so intense that even great and conventional ladies like old Lady Cadogan stood up on their little green chairs to catch a glimpse of her.

Mrs Langtry's conquest of fashionable Society in the late 1870s was sudden and overwhelming. The daughter of a priest in the Isle of Jersey, she married a widower with money and brought him to London, where they set

31 Hyde Park Corner in the 1850s. A carriage drive in the Park was an afternoon entertainment for the ladies of high birth and breeding who dominated the London Season

32 Rotten Row in 1886. Hyde Park was the open-air rendezvous of high Society in the Season, crowded with smart carriages, ladies and gentlemen on horseback and their fashionable friends parading up and down beside the Row

up an establishment in Eaton Place and with the help of Lord Ranelagh, whom she had known in Jersey, gained an entrée into the narrow world of Society. Wearing the same black dress every night and one diamond star in her hair, her beauty was so dazzling as she swept through the London drawing-rooms, with Mr Langtry trailing meekly behind her, that she made every other lady there look overdressed and fussy, and it was not surprising if the Prince of Wales was immediately captivated. He met her first at a small supper party and very soon it was common knowledge that he would go nowhere unless Mrs Langtry had also been invited. Well-bred hostesses were obliged to sink their pride and to obey the royal command. Princess Alexandra accepted the lady as a guest at Marlborough House and even Queen Victoria, overcome with the desire to see this alluring creature, made one of her rare appearances at a Buckingham Palace Drawing-Room when she knew her son had arranged for Mrs Langtry to be presented.

Her portrait was painted by Edward Poynter, Whistler, Burne-Jones and Millais, whose picture, entitled *The Jersey Lily*, created such a sensation at the Royal Academy Summer Exhibition it had to be roped off to keep the crowds at bay. But Mrs Langtry went a little too far in the end, even for the standards of morality at Marlborough House. There was Prince Louis of Battenberg, and there were rumours of other lovers; and by then Mr Langtry's purse was empty, so the Prince of Wales with the utmost kindness used his influence to put her on the stage. She was thus able to exchange one profession for another and to begin at the top of her theatrical career with no acting experience whatever. She also insisted on a red carpet being rolled out from her dressing-room into the wings at the Princess's Theatre, where she made her début as Shakespeare's serpent of old Nile in *Antony and Cleopatra*, lying on a leopard skin couch suitably smothered in real jewellery, which was insured for half a million pounds.

Such goings-on shocked the more modest and more sensible members of the upper classes, still faithful to their sorrowing Queen and all she represented. To them fashionable Society had become degenerate and the values they had lived by in the 1850s and 60s seemed to be threatened by a new materialism and a severe decline in morality. In 1870 when the heir to the throne was involved in the Mordaunt divorce case, admitting in his evidence that he was in the habit of taking a hansom cab when he wished to visit a

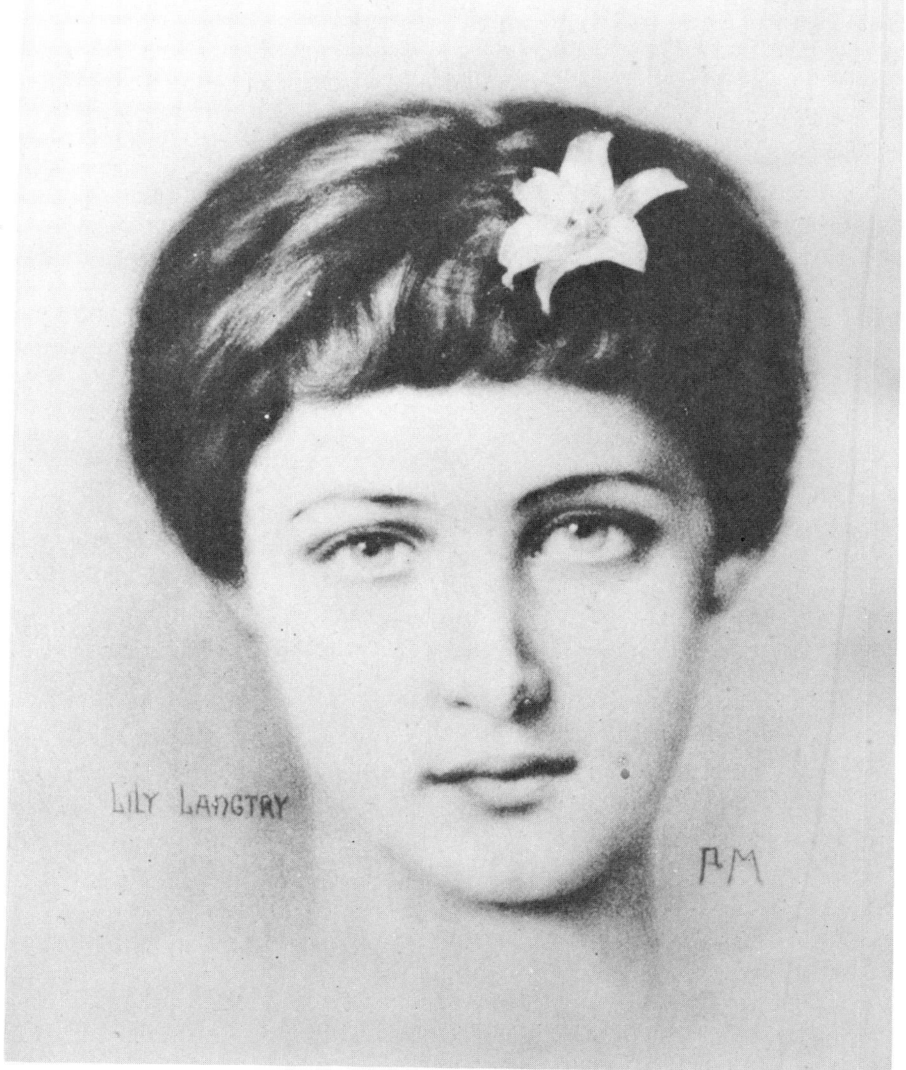

33 Lillie Langtry, the beautiful and calculating young woman from the Isle of Jersey, whose conquest of the Prince of Wales and London Society in the 1870s shocked the older members of the high aristocracy

friend incognito, eyebrows were raised in horror, and some years later the Tranby Croft case of cheating at cards created an even worse scandal. It proved only too well that the Prince of Wales was not over-sensitive about the company he kept and that vulgarity was to be found even among the highest in the land.

Mothers, anxious for their daughters' welfare, said the London Season was not what it had been. Yet there could be no return to what now seemed a more stable era in Society when the Queen and Prince Albert were young and their eldest son still in the hands of his tutors. All the Queen could do was to raise a huge memorial to her husband in Kensington Gardens as an example of a virtuous life dedicated to all that was good and chaste. It was designed by Gilbert Scott, who conceived the idea of erecting 'a kind of *ciborium*' or Gothic shrine, inlaid with precious metals, mosaics, enamel work and *alto-relievo* sculpture. Being a man of great piety, Mr Scott believed Providence had chosen him for this great work and he did not fail to achieve his mammoth task. The marble frieze alone, some 200 feet in length, contained 170 life-size figures and there were eight colossal marble statues illustrating the Christian and moral virtues, besides eight equally colossal bronzes representing the arts and sciences, with, of course, the seated figure of the Prince Consort, weighing some 10 tons and poised aloft under a star-studded canopy, as the final emblem of superiority.

The memorial was finished in 1876 and the Queen was so delighted, she gave Mr Scott a knighthood. But Society did not often penetrate as far as Kensington Gardens; it preferred the little green chairs in Hyde Park and the pageant of the rich, the elegant and the notorious riding or driving by at the height of the London Season.

4
Dinner Parties

Nothing was so hedged about with snobbery, etiquette and competitiveness as the dinner parties of Victorian Society; nothing caused the hostess so much agitation and anxiety. First she had to consider who would pair with whom and who should be asked as the guest of honour. At least one eminent gentleman should be invited – or, if there were two, great care had to be taken that they would not try to eclipse each other. If either, or both, were married, of course their wives, however dull, must also be asked. If not married, then a suitable lady had to be found to make up the numbers at the table – by no means an easy task, since ladies, other than those belonging to the family, were not expected to accept engagements without an escort and if they did, were labelled 'fast'.

Every hostess had her 'guest list' of people she considered worthy of her acquaintance: old friends and new friends, people she wished to cultivate for their distinction or wealth, or for the use they might be to her husband, and people who had to be paid back, cutlet for cutlet, for entertaining her. Mrs Jeune, in the very formal and confined society of Oxford University, found she had been very remiss on this account and wrote in her diary: 'In the case of the Blisses of Corpus it is *we* not *they* who have appeared to drop the acquaintance by not inviting them in turn, and now it is too late to mend the matter. Mrs Bliss, I know, is extremely punctilious about returning dinner for dinner, so I suppose we may consider them quite struck off our visiting-list.... The loss is certainly not very great,' she added rather acidly, though her assumption proved to be wrong, as a few weeks later the Blisses did invite her and Dr Jeune to another dinner party at Corpus Christi, the dinner 'very bad' and the company 'very dull'.

Twelve was considered a good number for a small dinner party, 20, 30 or anything up to 40 or 60 for a grander occasion, which had to be organized with a military precision if the evening was to be successful. Invitations were sent out on elaborately embossed invitation cards three weeks before the event and had to be accepted or declined within 24 hours. Once accepted, nothing short of a contagious illness or a bereavement could excuse the guest from attending – any other form of apology was ill-bred.

Bachelor men were much in demand if they were witty and good company, and the number of invitations they received confirmed their status in Society. Henry James, after the success of his novel *Daisy Miller*, dined out in London 107 times in the spring and summer of 1879. 'You will simply wonder what can have induced me to perpetrate such a folly and how I have survived to tell the tale!' he wrote to a friend in Cambridge; and although he meant 'to take in sail' for the rest of the Season, when it came to the point he accepted another 33 invitations. 'I couldn't keep out of it,' he went on, 'I had become a highly developed diner-out', for in spite of the ensuing interruptions, repetitions and fatigues being 'horribly wearisome' and making work 'extremely difficult', he could not resist the blandishments of all the ladies clamouring to entertain him. He had youth, good looks, good manners and a sensitivity that was rare among the Americans in London, so that he never put a foot wrong socially. Women liked him 'especially for his sympathetic and delicate discernment of their own nice qualities.' Sex was not their chief attraction for him; he set them up on a pedestal, which was extremely gratifying to their *amour-propre*, responding to 'a pronounced refinement' in them and treating them with great respect.

Self-esteem was important to Victorian high Society and behaviour at a dinner party strictly controlled by politeness. The host and hostess stood in

34 Dinner is served. The formal procession into the dining-room was drawn up in strict order of precedence, the host leading the way. George du Maurier

35 The dinner table at Grosvenor House laid for a banquet served by liveried footmen. A silver gilt plateau ran down the centre of the table supporting the gold vases, candelabra and alabaster statuary holding aloft dishes of fruit and flowers

the drawing-room to receive their guests, who were announced by the butler or a be-wigged footman. Introductions were made and the ladies invited to sit. No drinks were offered and no smoking was allowed. The ladies *en grande toilette* eyed each other with critical admiration, envy or barely concealed scorn. The gentlemen, in white ties and tails, eyed the ladies hopefully. It was permissible if you knew your hostess well enough to tell her she looked pretty, provided she was young and not too haughty to disdain a compliment; otherwise the light conversation suitable to the occasion rippled from one trivial topic to another. To arrive late or flustered was quite unforgivable.

The host undertook the solemn duty of telling each gentleman which lady he was to take in to dinner and when the butler announced that dinner was served, offered his arm to the senior lady present before leading the way into the dining-room. The other guests, strictly in order of precedence, followed in a procession like the pairs of animals entering the Ark, the hostess bringing up the rear with the senior gentleman. It was necessary to know the precise position of each guest in the social hierarchy if dangerous mistakes were to be avoided, and well nigh impossible to sit people together who might actually enjoy each other's company unless they were matched in rank and fortune. None the less many a romance did begin at the dinner table and was afterwards encouraged or nipped in the bud by the vigilant hostess.

Table decorations varied according to the wealth and grandeur of the host, the strong rooms of the nobility containing a mass of treasures in gold and silver, crystal, alabaster and ivory that were brought out for the occasion. When the Duke of Westminster entertained at Grosvenor House, a buffet at one end of the dining-room was covered with his vast collection of family gold plate, including several enormous antique salvers and a profusion of gold cups and vases won by the horses of his famous racing stable. A silver gilt plateau ran the whole length of the dining-table supporting an immense

36 A dinner party in 1890: the guests taking their seats at the elaborately decorated table, each place provided with a hand-written copy of the menu in a small silver frame

epergne of centaurs holding aloft a dish filled with flowers and greenery, with two large statuettes of naked men and rearing horses placed on either side of it, four giant urn-shaped vases and a number of branched candelabra all of glittering gold. Bowls and dishes of exotic fruit from Eaton Hall added to the sumptuous and dazzling effect, and no one who dined with the Duke seemed to think the display was overdone or in the least vulgar.

In fact, dinner parties of any size or distinction were a status symbol and a means of showing off. The centre of the table was always decorated with a fancy looking silver epergne with mermaids, goddesses or cherubs bearing improbable dishes of fruit and bon-bons, or little cups and vases filled with ferns. Candelabra were supported by bosomy caryatids with jewelled eyes, and candlesticks were made in the shape of lilies, harebells or ecclesiastical vessels with Gothic embellishments. Glass, dinner services, lace and linen napery and silver cutlery all suffered from the Victorian mania for a riot of ornamentation. The more expensive they looked, the better they were; and the middle classes, aping their betters, endeavoured not to be left behind. Kate Dickens, when she moved with her husband to Devonshire Terrace after he had become a figure in the literary world, covered her dinner table with quantities of artificial flowers. 'The very candles rose out of an artificial rose,' Jane Carlyle observed, 'and the profusion of figs, raisins and oranges absolutely overloaded the dessert.'

At the beginning of the century dinner was served *à la Française* with each course laid on the table in front of the host and hostess to be carved and handed round. Then it became fashionable to serve it *à la Russe*, which meant cutting up the dishes before they were brought to the table, so that they could be handed round more quickly and with less fuss. Either way the menu, always written in French, was long and very complicated, beginning with soup and fish, followed by removes or *relevés*, *flancs* or side dishes, *entrées*, a choice of roasts, *entremets de douceur*, savouries and dessert.

Two soups were offered, one thick and one clear and two sorts of fish: *Filets de Sole à la Bisque*, *Turbot à la Richelieu*, or perhaps *Saumon en Matelote Normande* or *Mayonnaise de Homard*. Then came the removes, large dishes served to look as appetizing as possible: *La Hanche de Venaison aux haricots verts*, *Les Poulardes en Diadème*, or some other form of poultry cooked in cream by the chef and garnished with vegetables. *Flancs* or side dishes and *entrées* were then brought to the table, covering a wide range of taste: *Côtelettes d'Agneau demi Provençale*, *Noix de Veau demi grasse à la purée de Concombres*, *Ortolans à la Vicomtesse*, *Vol-au-Vent de Fois Gras à la Talleyrand* and *Aiguillettes de petites Poussins à la Banquière*. And if none of these proved to be sufficiently satisfying, there was still the *pièce de résistance* to come: *Les Dindons Poults piqués et bardés, garnis de Cailles aux feuilles de vignes*, or *Les jeunes Levrauts au jus de groseilles* served with *petits pois à l'anglaise*.

Happily the guests were not expected to eat of every dish that was offered at the table. The *gourmets* could pick and choose, the guzzlers indulge their greed to the limit. If they survived so far, and the heavily corsetted ladies had to struggle manfully to do so, the *entremets* were comparatively soothing. Ices, soufflés, *bombes surprises, gateaux* and apricots or strawberries tossed in brandy, went down easily as a prelude to the final splendour of the dessert, when the table was cleared and the finger-bowls set in front of each guest with dishes of grapes, figs, nuts, apples, peaches and pineapples. One book of etiquette sensibly warned its readers 'to avoid embarking on an orange, as it requires long experience, a colossal courage, any amount of cool self-possession and a great skill to attack and dispose of one without harm to yourself or your neighbours.'

Towards the end of the dessert, the hostess 'collected eyes', indicating to the ladies that it was time for them to rise and follow her into the drawing-room — a delicate and difficult moment which had to be carefully timed. The gentlemen also rose, one of them holding the door open to usher the ladies out, before returning to the table and the decanters of port. But the heavy drinking habits of the Regency had become a thing of the past among the more sober Victorian gentlemen and it was not often that they lingered for very long in the dining-room. Prince Albert had disliked the kind of bawdy, masculine conversation that was permitted over the port and the Prince of Wales was always impatient to rejoin the ladies. Moreover his preference for drinking champagne was quickly followed by fashionable Society and it was only the connoisseurs who continued to appreciate a vintage port.

37 'Bereavement'. The ladies withdraw from the dining-room after the dessert, the hostess leading the way into the drawing-room. George du Maurier

38 The gentlemen get together over the vintage port to discuss politics and sport and to swap bawdy stories at the table of a *nouveau-riche* host. George du Maurier

Catering on a large scale depended on a number of people in the household acting on the instructions of the head steward. Provisions were sent up to London by rail from the country, especially the exotic fruits and vegetables, the game, venison, poultry and meat, shot or grown on the estates of the territorial grandees; and with only very primitive forms of refrigeration, the larders and store houses alongside the kitchen groaned with every sort and kind of food. Yet at home the dinner table in some households was not always very generously furnished. Lady Stanley, staying at Eaton Hall in the time of the Duke of Westminster's very rich and very tight-fisted father, said the evenings were very disagreeable. 'The 1st night the Cheshire Militia came to dinner and the next, 2 quite unknown young men who sat on the edges of their chairs and got no food — and what food — I must say that passes all belief. Fancy each help of fish being *half* a sprat and the 8th part of a boiled sole and the drumsticks of a fowl being handed all round.... Really the whole affair was ludicrous.'

Dinner at Blenheim with the Duke and Duchess of Marlborough could be no more enjoyable. Mrs Jeune and her husband were summoned there with the Dean of Christchurch and Mrs Liddell one very cold November night in 1858. 'Furs and hot water bottles kept us warm and prevented any evil results,' she wrote, but it was a dull evening. Lord Shaftesbury, who was placed between the Duchess and Mrs Jeune, talked very little, and 'the

Duchess sat evidently racking her brains for some subject of conversation, but was unsuccessful in finding any sufficiently interesting to excite more than a sentence or two from either of her supporters.' She seemed 'neither clever nor at all handsome', and the Duke also in Mrs Jeune's opinion was 'a plain man in all its meanings', though she thought it was 'in itself an immense merit to be a religious Duke of Marlborough', adding ungrammatically, 'and this His Grace has.'

39 Mr Gladstone dines at Haddo House with Lord and Lady Aberdeen and the Earl of Rosebery, while a Scottish piper entertains them with a little music. A. E. Emslie

Perhaps Mrs Jeune was rather hard to please. At another dinner party in Oxford she was very disappointed in Mr Gladstone because he hogged the conversation, and all the men at the table concentrated on listening to him instead of making themselves agreeable to the ladies sitting next to them. Mrs Gladstone – 'a fine, fashionable woman' – also behaved in a very odd and high-handed manner, disappearing after the ladies had left the table and not returning to the drawing-room until the gentlemen came upstairs.

This was one of the most difficult moments of a successful dinner party. If the gentlemen stayed too long over their port, the ladies got tired of making trivial conversation among themselves. Caroline Jebb – or Cara as she was known by her family – the attractive American wife of the Professor of Greek at Cambridge, had her own tactics on such occasions. At a dinner party in Edinburgh, she sat between two law lords – 'much more interesting than lords by birth' – and was so delighted with their conversation she was determined to avoid 'the nooks by the fireside' when the ladies retired to the drawing-room, 'holding her ground' with another lady 'by cordially but firmly keeping up the conversation *standing*', so that she could choose a seat accessible to the men when they came upstairs. 'I am not going to talk to old tabbies this evening with a lot of clever men to listen to,' she declared afterwards, and sure enough Professor Messon, who talked about women's rights, Professor Geikie, a geologist, and her two law lords all gathered round her, and sooner or later every gentleman in the room was presented, showing, as she complacently added, 'the great advantage it is to have a good position in the drawing-room.'

40 Coffee and tea in the drawing-room after dinner. Flirting enlivened the boredom of polite conversation and gossip, and sentiment was sweetly expressed by a downcast eye

Lady Jebb, as she became when her husband was knighted, was very much the queen of Cambridge society. Like so many American women, she was full of vitality and had a flair for twisting people around her little finger. With bright auburn hair, a Rubensesque countenance and a deep rich voice, she created a sensation in the quiet drawing-rooms of the university professors and was quite unlike any of their wives. The first dinner party she gave as a young bride with very little money to spend was an outstanding success. She arranged the table herself, filling the epergne with artificial flowers so cleverly mixed with laurel and spruce no one could guess they were not real, and by saving on the expense of fresh flowers, she was able to hire two

waiters to help Martin, the butler, and a girl to help Mrs Bird in the kitchen. An excellent cook on a wage of £20 a year, Mrs Bird was evidently a 'treasure'. 'I left the preparations of most of the dinner to her, simply giving my orders, and everything was perfect,' Cara wrote to her American relations after the event. 'Mrs Bird made the rolls herself (one is laid at each plate, you know, instead of bread. She makes excellent rolls). Then she made white soup, fried twelve fillets of sole and made the lobster sauce to go with the fish. Next we had two entrées ordered from the College ... the first "timballes de foie gras" and then "sweetbreads stewed with mushrooms and truffles". With these Mrs Bird had nothing to do, which gave her breathing time to dish the main dinner. She roasted the leg of mutton, boiled the turkey, made its sauce of oysters, and cooked all the vegetables, potatoes, cauliflower and celery, which go with this course. When we were through with this, she sent up the roast duck with its sauce.... Then we had plum pudding from the College and after that Charlotte Russe, then cheese ... and then the table was cleared for dessert. All the wine glasses, decanters etc. were taken off, the crumbs brushed away, and then new decanters put on and dessert plates. The waiters then handed round one dish after another of the dessert, after which we ladies arose and left the room to the gentlemen.'

Dick Jebb was an affable host and congratulated his wife on the success of her first dinner party, so that she went on to tell her American relations that 'entertaining here is a great pleasure and no trouble to the hostess. After

41 'Maidenhood and Sirenhood' by R. Loudon. After dinner in the drawing-room the experienced ladies attract the admiration of the gentlemen while the younger ladies are neglected

dinner we played games and to crown all, there was a row among the cabmen outside who got tired of waiting for the guests to go away.' But this was only one of many very enjoyable dinner parties at the Jebbs' house. Cara was an indefatigable matchmaker and as she grew older, persuaded a succession of lively and attractive American nieces to stay with her in Cambridge, all of whom she tried to inveigle into matrimony with the upper-class English undergraduates she invited to dinner.

There was Gerald Balfour, with an income of £1000 a year, in Cara's opinion 'the most superior man I ever met ... can call cousins with half the nobility of England', an ideal match, she thought, for her niece, Nellie Dupuy. At a dinner party which brought them together, Nellie wore a green cashmere dress belonging to her Aunt, 'made in the aesthetic Greek style', and a little blue plush jacket; but she failed to respond to Balfour's lofty, intellectual spirit, which led her Aunt to the conclusion that 'it is as hard to love up as to love down.' Poor Nellie returned to Philadelphia without a husband and was succeeded by her sister, Maud, who found Cambridge society 'the Utopia of all my fondest dreams'. She thought Gerald Balfour 'just what you would imagine an English Lord to look and be like — he is so beautiful.' But it was one of Charles Darwin's sons, George, who, with her Aunt's connivance, always contrived to sit next to her at dinner, and George Darwin who eventually won her heart with Aunt Cara's full approval.

As a hostess, Lady Jebb was charming and witty, if at times somewhat unconventional. But a touch of eccentricity was accepted in academic circles and also much admired in the more Bohemian society of the successful writers and artists who gathered around Mrs Thoby Prinsep at Little Holland House in Kensington in the 1850s. She was one of the beautiful and unconventional Pattle sisters, daughters of an Indian civil servant and his French wife, and a lion-hunter, ambitious to create a salon in London for the distinguished men and women of her acquaintance. Her husband had made a considerable fortune in Anglo-Indian trade before retiring to England and standing for Parliament and was thus able to indulge his wife's desire to shine as a hostess and to ignore the malicious gossip her parties sometimes engendered. For Sara Prinsep offered something different from the conventional dinner parties of Victorian society. She kept open house on Sunday afternoons in the summer when Sunday everywhere else was a day of gloom and pious boredom, inviting her guests to stroll about the lawns or from room to room in the rambling, 'artistic' house and keeping the most favoured to dinner, which on warm nights was served in the garden at a long table under the trees.

G. F. Watts, the painter, occupied a studio in the garden; he came on a two-day visit and stayed for 25 years, endlessly painting the Pattle sisters in the romantic disguise of biblical handmaidens or Ellen Terry, his innocent child bride of a few month's duration, in the flowing draperies of a Renaissance princess. Holman Hunt, Dante Gabriel Rossetti, Burne-Jones and Ruskin were all guests at Little Holland House at one time or another, with Tennyson, Browning, Carlyle, Thackeray, Benjamin Jowett and Disraeli. Those who did not receive an invitation sneered at 'Mrs Prinsep's tea-gardens' and mocked at the subservience of 'Dog Thoby' to his wife's whims. Those who gathered on the lawns on Sunday afternoon and were fortunate enough to be asked to stay to dinner, waxed lyrical in praise of their dynamic hostess and the brilliant conversation 'enlivened by the wit of cynics, the dreams of the inspired and the thoughts of the profoundest thinkers of the age.'

Julia Margaret Cameron, the most talented of the Pattle sisters, pursued Sara's distinguished guests round the garden with her camera, begging them to sit for her with such insistence few of them were brave enough to refuse. Garcia sang after dinner, Joachim, Piatti and Hallé played chamber music; and as Holman Hunt declared: 'Nowhere else in England would it have been possible to enter a house with such a singular variety of beautiful persons inhabiting it.' Not that his enthusiasm was shared by everyone — for when Virginia, the most beautiful of the sisters, married the son and heir of Earl Somers, a comparatively new peer, Lady Elizabeth Spencer-Stanhope was reported to have said: 'It will be curious to watch her rise, as I believe she is *not yet* in good Society.'

Lady Elizabeth's haughty air of aristocratic superiority was by no means unique in the 1850s, and as time went on, 'good' Society and fashionable Society became still more divided. The first was exclusive and loyal to the respectable Queen; the second had become less so by the 1870s, owing to the gregarious instincts of the Prince of Wales and his love of pleasure. His appetite for the good things of life, and for rich food in particular, appeared to be unlimted. Even his long suffering wife said it was 'terrible' the amount of food he could eat at a dinner party. He set the fashion for swallowing several dozen oysters between mouthfuls of brown bread and butter in a matter of minutes and was impatient with anyone who dallied too long over a dish or played around with it. He liked caviare, plovers' eggs, ortolans and soles poached in Chablis, garnished with oysters and prawns. Chicken and turkey in aspic, quails packed with *foie gras*, pheasants stuffed with truffles, woodcock, snipe, grouse and game pie were among his favourite dishes; and in 1890 when Escoffier created a *specialité* for him called *Cuisses des Nymphes à l'Aurore* consisting of frogs' thighs served cold in a jelly made of cream and Moselle flavoured with paprika, he relished every mouthful.

Entertaining His Royal Highness put his friends to a great deal of trouble and cost them a lot of money. But the Rothschilds owned houses in London as luxurious as their palatial mansions in the Vale of Aylesbury and once again family solidarity kept them all together in a cluster round the Hyde Park end of Piccadilly, which was known as Rothschild Row. Natty lived at 148 Piccadilly, next to Apsley House, Hannah Rosebery at 107, Ferdinand at 143 and his sister, Alice, at 142. Anthony's widow, Louise, lived round the corner at 19 Grosvenor Gate, Leo at 5 Hamilton Place and Alfred at 1 Seamore Place. All of them were incredibly generous and their dinner parties were the most magnificent in London. The finest wines and the finest food cooked by the celebrated French chefs they employed, appeared on the table and it was nothing for the ladies to find some exquisite jewelled ornament wrapped in the lace napkin beside their places. Mrs Langtry, however, was too greedy at one of Alfred's 'adoration dinners' when it was his custom to invite one particularly alluring lady to dine alone with him and three or four other gentlemen. As he drew her aside towards the end of the evening and murmured: 'What shall I give you, beautiful lady?' she calmly turned and picked up a fabulous Louis XVI bejewelled snuff box and said: 'This will do.' 'He had a weak heart,' she wrote later, 'and for the moment I thought I had stopped it. But when he got his breath he promised me something "much prettier" and out came one of the well-known gift boxes.' The rapacious lady was not exactly overjoyed — as a professional beauty her price was high.

First class French chefs were also at a premium during this extravagant period, but they had one great rival in a lively and quite extraordinary young Englishwoman called Rosa Ovenden. Born in Essex in 1867 she started life as a maid of all work at the age of twelve, educating herself through reading the old newspapers her middle-class mistress threw out for lighting the fires. Pictures of the beautiful women like Lady Randolph Churchill who moved in fashionable Society with such grace and elegance and reports of the dinners and receptions they attended, kindled Rosa's imagination; and before long, without saying a word to her family, she found herself a new

42 Foreign musicians were engaged to entertain the guests after dinner, but much to their dismay, the guests often went on chattering loudly through the music. George du Maurier

situation very much higher up the social ladder with the exiled Comte and Comtesse de Paris at Sheen House, Mortlake.

This household was at the centre of the very highest French society and although Rosa was only a humble kitchen maid earning 12s 6d a week, she was proud and happy to be working in such an illustrious milieu. Quick and witty, she soon picked up enough French to be able to hold her own among the staff and by watching the chef assiduously, to learn by degrees the whole art of *cordon bleu* cookery. Whether the story she told was true or not, she was supposed to have deputized for the chef on one occasion when the Prince of Wales was a guest at Sheen House, so that when he enquired, as he often did, if he might congratulate the cook on the excellent meal he had just eaten, he was astonished to be confronted by a very handsome young girl with vivid forget-me-not blue eyes, a plait of thick dark hair and a cockney accent. Quite unabashed she gave him a broad smile and a quick curtsey as he pulled out a little purse full of gold coins and pressed one into her hand, with the gallant quip: 'A sovereign, my dear, from your future Sovereign.'

It may well have been the first time Rosa had pleased His Royal Highness; it was certainly not the last. When she left Sheen at the age of 20 to try her luck in London, she went to cook for Lady Randolph Churchill whenever the resident chef was off duty. The heroine of the newspapers she had devoured in her attic bedroom at Leyton proved to be even more dazzling than Rosa had imagined and the two young women, so far apart in the social scale, took a fancy to each other. The dinner parties they concocted together were so successful Rosa became the talk of fashionable Society, and since she never lost her cockney wit or her high spirits, she soon made a reputation as a 'character' as well as a cook. People started clamouring for her services and she charged accordingly, travelling from one rich house to another with her chef's cap, spotless white overall and special high-laced cooking boots, which were made to measure from the finest leather to support her legs during the long hours she spent standing in the kitchen.

When it became known that the Prince of Wales found her attractive and preferred her cooking to any other, Rosa was in greater demand than ever. Her presence inthe kitchen was a guarantee of royal favour and any hostess could rest comfortably on the prospect of giving a really successful dinner party. Rosa knew the likes and dislikes of everyone in Society. She knew who could not eat lobster patties because shell fish brought them out in spots and how the Prince liked plain boiled truffles served in a silver dish wrapped in a white linen napkin. And if anything went wrong, which was seldom, her powers of improvization were as brilliant as her capacity for swearing as loudly as a Billingsgate fishwife and then suddenly bursting into peals of Rabelaisian laughter.

When she was 25 Rosa married a butler called Excelsior Lewis and this was the only big mistake she ever made. For a time they ran a superior boarding-house in Eaton Terrace, Rosa continuing her free-lance catering from her own kitchen and hiring a number of young women to help her. Up at 5 a.m. to do her own marketing, she prepared some of the dishes at home and after collecting her young women together in a cab, set off for her client's house in the afternoon, taking over the kitchen there to prepare and serve the dinner in the evening. Only the best and most expensive ingredients went into her dishes, and if anyone was foolish enough to complain of her extravagance, she put a black mark against the house and never returned. She could pick and choose and did not hesitate to show who was master of the situation. But meanwhile, Excelsior Lewis, perhaps in self-defence, had taken to the bottle, and when they moved to the Cavendish Hotel in Jermyn Street with a big, airy kitchen more suitable for Rosa's catering operations, she booted him out.

By then she was the absolute queen of caterers and the Prince who had given the cockney kitchen maid her first sovereign, was King. But another revolution in the eating habits of Society had also taken place in the 1890s, for with the development of the large, luxury hotels in London it suddenly became fashionable and a novelty for ladies to dine out in a public restaurant. Previously it was quite unheard of and no one who was not travelling from one place to another would have dreamed of doing such a thing. Restaurants anyway were glorified chop houses only suitable for men, or Soho supper rooms which no respectable lady would think of entering. Even Romano's and Kettner's were dubious, and it was not until the opening of the Savoy Hotel in 1889 that the idea of a well-bred lady eating out became possible.

Built by D'Oyly Carte on the money he had coined from the Gilbert and Sullivan operas, the Savoy was the last word in splendour, and with Cesar Ritz as the *maître d'hôtel* and Escoffier in the kitchen, nothing more could be desired. Soon it was discovered that eating out was more impromptu and more fun than the extensive and often boring dinner parties given at home – especially on Sundays when the servants had their time off. At first, Lady de Grey, a pioneer in fashionable Society, insisted on having a screen round her table at the Savoy to protect her party from the public gaze; but before long the screens were set aside and the rich and up-to-date hedonists were to be seen in increasing numbers enjoying the *haute cuisine* and the elegant service of the restaurant overlooking the river. Other hoteliers cashed in – the mammoth Hotel Cecil was built next to the Savoy, the Metropole and the Grand in Northumberland Avenue and the Carlton in the Haymarket, where Ritz and Escoffier, after their dismissal from the Savoy, created the most distinguished restaurant in London patronized by the Prince of Wales and the *crème de la crème* of Society. '*Le client a toujours raison,*' Ritz once observed, '*mais il paie toujours*', and as money was no object among his clients, he served them well, understood their foibles and gave them everything they wanted.

5
The Gentlemen

In the first 30 years of Queen Victoria's long reign gentlemen aspired to an ideal type of manhood – serious, conscientious and morally impeccable. In the last 30 years, these virtues, so rigorously imitated by the middle classes, became less attractive to high Society, though they still governed the outward behaviour of the majority of upper-class Englishmen. It was necessary to be a good sport and a good loser, never to cheat at cards or on the racecourse, to uphold the honour of a gentleman at home and abroad, and to keep any sexual deviation from the straight and narrow path of domesticity very well covered. Only thus could the immense power and prestige of the nation and the Empire be maintained, only thus could the ruling aristocracy survive against the rising tide of democracy.

Fortunately the instinct for survival among the leading aristocratic families was very strong indeed, and many of them were sensitive enough to see the need for adapting themselves to the changing forces of the nineteenth century. Trained as they were to govern and to lead, they had a quality of dash and style the bourgeoisie reluctantly admired and by adopting a stricter code of morality than their predecessors they succeeded in retaining much of the power and privilege enjoyed by their ancestors.

There was, however, a very real danger of revolution in the 1840s. The working classes in town and country were wretchedly poor and hungry and the middle classes ambitious for more power. An arrogant, frivolous and worldly aristocracy paying no heed to its obligations towards the rest of the nation could well have been toppled. The French Revolution was still within living memory and the countries of Europe and the Near East beset by anarchy, disruption and internal strife. Only the English genius for compromise, combined with the flexibility and good example set by the governing class, gave a much needed stability to the people of Britain, so that by 1862 the Rev. Charles Kingsley was able to declare somewhat sententiously: 'There is no aristocracy in the world and there never has been, as far as I know, which has so honourably repented and brought forth fruits meet for repentance; which has so cheerfully asked what its duty was, that it might do it.... The whole creed of our young gentlemen is becoming more liberal, their demeanour more courteous, their language more temperate. They enquire after the welfare, or at least mingle in the sports of the working man, with a simple cordiality which was unknown thirty years ago.'

This 'noble change' in the attitude of the upper classes Kingsley believed was due to the influence of religion, both Evangelical and Anglican, to the spread of liberal principles 'founded on common humanity and justice', and to the example of a Court, 'virtuous, humane and beneficient'. It was also the reaction from one generation to another, a swing away from the idle, extravagant self-indulgence of George IV as Regent and King towards a more sober realization of life's seriousness. Thus the dissolute, spendthrift Marlboroughs produced the devout and respectable 7th Duke and the arrogant Marquess of Salisbury the more thoughtful and broad-minded Lord Robert Cecil.

As young men, both of them were strongly influenced by the High Church Tractarian Movement while studying at Oxford and found its rituals emotionally and spiritually satisfying. The sacrament brought them into direct contact with the Almighty and to partake of this beneficial experience it was necessary to cultivate a way of life in which chastity and modesty predominated and vice was held at bay. Neither Marlborough nor Lord Cecil as it happened had any taste for gambling or amorous adventure; but whereas Marlborough had a dull and somewhat self-righteous character, Lord Robert was intellectually brilliant and possessed a robust, ironic sense of humour, which became even more pronounced as he grew older giving his habitual air of patrician aloofness a sudden and attractive gleam of mischief. In his old age, bald and bearded and immensely stout, he took to riding a tricycle in the grounds of Hatfield. There, in the full-skirted frock coat and spats he wore at 10 Downing Street, he was to be seen astride this creaking vehicle, having been heaved into the saddle by two or three grandchildren who pushed energetically from behind.

Cambridge University had its equivalent to the Oxford Movement in the Apostles and the Ecclesiologists and was a hotbed of religious controversy in the 1840s. The Ecclesiologists concerned themselves with what they believed to be the correct form of worship in the High Church, studying in great detail the ecclesiastical records of the past and reviving the forgotten ritual of the Middle Ages. The Apostles, equally uncompromising in their devotion to the High Church, had a wider scope of influence and inspired the idealistic young undergraduates who had left the rough and tumble of their schooldays behind with a new cult of chivalry. The Duke of Rutland's son, Lord John Manners, was the leader of this crusade designed to give its valiant members faith in God, a courtly reverence to women as the weaker sex, a benevolent attitude towards their inferiors and a manly strength to battle against evil. Like the legendary knights of King Arthur's Round Table, the Apostles also honoured friendship as the elixir of life, earnestly linking arms as they strolled by the Cam in the evenings and debated the future of mankind.

Writing to his former tutor, William Brookfield, young George Lyttelton described his first impressions of life at Cambridge. 'We smoke – we read –

we become unsocial and narrow-minded — we feel romantic.... We drink Gesserheim — we pay reluctant Sunday visits to Lord Braybrooke [at Audley End] — we talk of books — we feel like a Fellow — we walk across the grass — we look at our fair ladies the which you may remember in our study — we are pious — we are worldly and amibitious....' But all the time George Lyttelton was working very hard at his classical studies. He won the Craven Scholarship in his first year and came out top of the Classical Tripos; and his love of learning was genuine, not at all an affectation or a shallow means of acquiring academic honours. He was steeped in the lore of Greece and Rome and yet, like so many of his contemporaries, the insight his scholarship gave him into other more pagan civilizations in no way shook his firm belief in the most dogmatic assertions of the Christian faith. Religion remained the central force of his life. After a day's hunting, if he returned in time for the evening service, he could be seen striding up the knave of Hagley Church with a dark overcoat thrown over his hunting pink, that was almost, but not quite, long enough to conceal his muddy boots.

His father died soon after he left Cambridge and as the 4th Baron Lyttelton, he inherited Hagley Hall near Birmingham, a Palladian house with a beautiful garden and an estate that yielded very little money. Undeterred by this he paid court to Mary Glynne, whose sister, Catherine, already engaged to W. E. Gladstone, pressed her to accept him. Dazed with joy when she did accept his proposal in the drawing-room of the Glynnes' house in Berkeley Square, the young man hurried down the stairs and was seized by Gladstone waiting in the room below, who pulled him down on his knees so that together they might give thanks to Almighty God.

43 George, 4th Baron Lyttelton and his wife Mary, née Glynne. They had 12 children, were devoted to their family and lived on the Lyttelton estate at Hagley Hall, near Birmingham

The marriage was a happy one. Lyttelton failed to achieve the brilliant political career that his Cambridge tutor had predicted for him, perhaps because he was too uncompromising and, unlike his equally high-minded brother-in-law, had no real instinct for politics. When Gladstone got him an appointment as Under Secretary of the Colonial Office, he offended the senior civil servants in the department by correcting their grammar and altering their drafts without consulting them; and he was not much more successful as Chairman of the Commission of Endowed Schools. None the less he was very conscientious in attending to his duties as Chairman of the Board of Guardians and of the Training Schools in Birmingham, and an enthusiastic member of the committee set up by his friend Lord John Manners to introduce Sisterhoods in the Anglican Church.

All this charitable work was voluntary and while his wife worried about the grocers' bills, he gave his time as well as a great deal of financial assistance he could not really afford to any number of worthy causes. The arrival of 12 children — four girls and eight boys — taxed the Lytteltons' slender resources more than ever; but they adored their children and, like the vast majority of Victorian husbands, it never seemed to occur to George that his wife's delicate health had anything to do with bearing so many offspring. Only when she died after giving birth to the Benjamin of the family did he wonder briefly if she could have been saved, and by then it was too late. Plunged into one of his worst attacks of depression and despair he attempted to assuage his grief by writing a very long memorial covering every moment of Mary's last, agonizing days, when the whole family watched and prayed by her bedside in a prolonged ordeal the younger children were never to forget. Finally they were all taken to see their mother in her coffin, every blind in the house was drawn down and the great armorial hatchment hoisted over the hall door until the day of the funeral, when the girls clad in black silk frocks trimmed with crepe, and the boys with mourning bands round their hats, walked hand in hand in pairs to Hagley Church behind their sorrowing father.

Yet it would be wrong to see Lord Lyttelton as a pious, psalm-smiting paterfamilias revelling in an orgy of grief; he was merely following the fashion of his time in mourning his dead wife with all the trappings of woe considered respectful on such occasions. And although Bible reading and almost daily attendance at church formed the background of life at Hagley Hall, he was a devoted husband and never an autocratic parent. His sons and daughters admired his moral rectitude and loved him for his high-spirited gaiety, which so suddenly alternated with his moods of black depression. They welcomed his second marriage 12 years later to the widowed daughter of a neighbouring landowner, who gave him three more children, and were distressed when his melancholia increased as he grew older and they could no longer tease him out of what they called his 'grubous' moods. Sadly, even with his deep religious convictions, life became quite unbearable to him in the end, and rushing out of his bedroom one morning, he threw himself over the banisters into the well of the staircase below.

Lord Lyttelton was by no means unique in suffering from the strange dichotomy that bedevilled so many Victorian gentlemen. On the surface they appeared to be successful, high-minded, rather complacent and very sure of themselves. Yet beneath their bewhiskered and dignified appearance, many of them were plagued with doubts and a sense of sin. The churches they built and the schools they endowed to bring their weaker brethren into the fold, were also a witness to the need they felt for saving their own souls and for quieting the conscience that stirred so uncomfortably at the back of their minds. They felt it was their duty to believe in progress, 'in the fulfilment of the great and sacred mission God had given to man to perform in this world' and, as it seemed, to Englishmen in particular. They felt they had a moral obligation to guide their wives and children towards a virtuous life, and that it was their business to teach the lower orders to love God and respect their betters. But the ways of doing so were sometimes hard and narrow and strewn with boulders. For 30 years Lord Lyttelton taught in the Sunday School at Hagley and only when he gave it up, admitted that he had not enjoyed doing it at all. Then at one time he was doubtful about installing his brother in the rectorship at Hagley, because Billy had gone to Germany after his ordination and while there had imbibed the dangerous Lutheran Low Church doctrine, which was anathema to George. Fortunately brother affection and the common practice among landowners of granting the livings at their disposal to a member of the family prevailed and the Dowager Lady Lyttelton wrote a soothing and tactful letter to George. 'We are indeed living in sad times as to Church matters', she declared. 'Dire schisms splitting every parish and family into sects, and infesting every plan, book, conversation and sermon — I trust real religion will not suffer in the scuffle.'

It often did. The Oxford Movement led to the conversion — or perversion as some preferred to call it — of many earnest souls to the Church of Rome; and when Archdeacon Manning followed Newman's example in 1851, a cry of dismay went through the upper-class drawing-rooms in London and the country, his lapse being all the more regrettable because this tall, ascetic-looking churchman with a thin-lipped smile and penetrating eyes, belonged to the best circles. Educated at Harrow and at Oxford, his advance from curate to rector and archdeacon had been swift, if at times a little devious. He had an instinct for mixing with the right people and a personality that inspired men and women to adore him and to seek his help and guidance in their spiritual problems. The shock of his conversion was therefore all the more violent and agonizing to his Protestant friends, especially to Gladstone, who described it as 'altogether the severest blow that ever befell me.' He could not at first believe it. 'Popery' was devilry to the devout followers of the Anglican Church and the Vatican, with its opulent priests living on the fat of the land, an institution they believed should have been suppressed centuries ago. That the English bishops also lived on the fat of the land was quite beside the point; they belonged to the hierarchy of the Anglican community and as such were less open to criticism.

Manning himself had been earmarked for a bishopric before his conscience cautioned him to throw aside all thoughts of worldly success to save his soul in the one and only true faith. He did not, however, remain a humble priest in the Church of Rome for long. In less than 15 years he had again swiftly and silently reached the top, succeeding Cardinal Wiseman as Archbishop of Westminster and so attaining absolute power over the Catholic community in Britain. Gladstone never quite forgave him. He, also, could be notoriously devious and inscrutable in his dealings with his political colleagues, but in his abiding faith in the Anglican Church he was a man of principle and in the circumstances he felt it was necessary to sacrifice the friendship which had meant so much to him. 'Our differences, my dear Archbishop, are indeed profound,' he wrote. 'We refer them I suppose in humble silence to a Higher Power.... You assured me once of your prayers at all and the most solemn times. I received that assurance with gratitude and

44 Cardinal Manning, whose conversion to the Church of Rome in 1851 dismayed all his Anglican friends and to the high-minded, fiercely Protestant Gladstone, was 'the severest blow' that had ever befallen him. G. F. Watts

still cherish it. As and when they move upwards, there is a meeting point for those whom a chasm separates below.'

Such differences in religious belief troubled many a Victorian gentleman and even those who were not disturbed by the theological problems of Manning and Gladstone were deeply shocked and disorientated by the publication in 1859 of Charles Darwin's *Origin of Species,* which turned the Book of Genesis into a fairy story and gave mankind a terrible new significance. None the less, attendance at church on Sunday mornings continued to be strictly observed. The gentlemen, suitably dressed in tall hats and frock coats, walked a little ahead of their wives swathed in rich folds of silk and satin and their children in tight button boots and tiny kid gloves. They arrived when all the rest of the congregation was seated and took their place in the family pew, and after the service was over, they lingered a moment or two to talk to the clergy and some of their neighbours. They were on good terms with the bishop and the bishop's lady, gradually moving down the hierarchic scale through the archdeacons to the vicars and the curates, who were sometimes invited to tea at the big house or for a talk in the study.

Sunday was a day of rest, a day of non-pleasure for everyone: no games for the children, no books and newspapers for the adults, only letter-writing or a post-prandial snooze in private, Bible reading and a cold supper in the evening to allow the upper servants time off to go to church. Faith had to be observed – and indeed faith was observed with great solemnity; but it did not always meet with a just reward. The Duke of Marlborough failed to instil the rudiments of virtue and morality into his eldest son, Blandford, who left

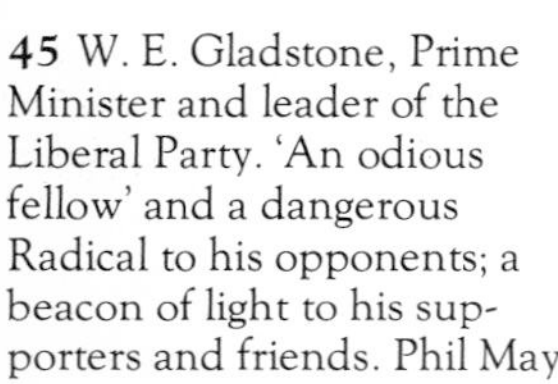

45 W. E. Gladstone, Prime Minister and leader of the Liberal Party. 'An odious fellow' and a dangerous Radical to his opponents; a beacon of light to his supporters and friends. Phil May

his wife for Lady Aylesford and when his wife divorced him, abandoned Lady Aylesford to marry a rich American widow, who was no lady at all. The Duke of Westminster was forced to ignore the infidelities of his beautiful first wife, Constance, and to pay the gambling debts of his sons; for whatever the Rev. Charles Kingsley may have thought or said, it was not easy for the upper classes to resist temptation. Did not the Bible say: 'Render unto Caesar the things that are Caesar's and unto God the things that are God's'? And the upper classes were Caesar. They made the rules and could bend them to suit their own convenience.

Moreover gentlemen had a great advantage over the ladies — they were a law unto themselves. Born to rule and to take an active part in worldly affairs, the paterfamilias in his own home expected to be feared and admired as the final authority and the fount of wisdom. He looked for obedience from his wife and children and indeed had absolute control over his wife's property, so that if he wanted to he could insist on her subservience. He demanded privacy within the four walls of his study and sympathy when he was ill or in trouble. But outside the feminine sphere of domesticity in what was essentially a masculine world of politics, business or pleasure, he would accept no interference from his wife or anyone else.

Lady Stanley adored her husband and undoubtedly he was very fond of her, yet he thought nothing of gadding about in Scotland at shooting parties to which she had not been invited, leaving her at Alderley to cope with their nine children and all the affairs of the household for two or three months at a time. 'I am sorry you still are fretted and in suspense about Scotland,' her mother-in-law wrote sympathetically. 'But I hope you will make use of the proverb "What can't be cured must be endured" — and above all that you will recollect unless it is given up cheerfully, you would be no *gainer* by keeping near you a discontented being who had only given way to importunity — you must make the best of it and the only comfort you can have is the thorough sympathy of your friends and the consciousness that you have kept a steady upright course yourself, anxious to do your duty as wife and mother. I most deeply pity Alderley and you, that present times are not like past times when all pleasure and happiness was looked for at *home*.'

Poor Lady Stanley tried very hard to follow her mother-in-law's advice, but on one occasion when she had heard nothing from her husband for weeks and suspected that he had put off his return from Black Mount because 'that horrid woman Lady Jocelyn' was there, she could contain her anxiety no longer. 'Pray write to me and tell me who you are with,' she begged him. 'I feel quite lost without you and know nothing of you.' Lord Stanley replied from a shooting lodge at Glen Quoich, saying he had not written before because he did not know whether to send a letter to Alderley or to London. He described the stag hunting at Glen Quoich at great length and did not mention Lady Jocelyn at all, but ended his letter: 'Pray be reasonable and not always discovering mare's nests.' He then went on to Perth and did not return home until the end of October for a brief visit before going off again to stay with Lady Ashburton at the Grange. His wife wisely did not try to keep him against his will. 'You were so amiable in your transient visit, that you quite gladdened my heart,' she wrote. 'All seems bright when your face shines. I might certainly avoid distressing you sometimes and I will try. Amuse yourself well and come back happy.' Lady Jocelyn, it seems, had been forgotten.

Lord Stanley was a forthright, broad-minded character with a sardonic wit, loyal to his friends and keenly interested in the ebb and flow of politics. As a friend and supporter of Palmerston he took office as President of the Board of Trade and later as Postmaster General. But he detested 'putting forward personal pretensions and personal claims' and despised the manoeuvres of some of his colleagues to obtain the plums in the Cabinet. In the ministerial crisis of 1855 following the outbreak of the Crimean War, he thought Lord John Russell had behaved very badly, the Duke of Newcastle was greedy and incompetent and Lord Aberdeen had acted like a silly old woman. 'These personal quarrels do not redound to the credit of England and will throw discredit on our institutions,' he declared. 'More than one despotic monarch in Europe will chuckle over the difficulties produced by Parliamentary Government.' Yet he was a staunch defender of the parliamentary system and although too shrewd to be taken in and too cynical to have any illusions about public life, he enjoyed every minute of it. His recipe for the fatigues of office was 'a gossamer meal of cold chicken eaten late at night with his feet in a basin of hot water and a stupid novel to compose his mind for slumber.'

Stanley hated religiosity and humbug, often accusing 'that odious fellow' Gladstone of both, and objecting very strongly to his budget of 1860, which introduced a direct income tax of ten pence in the pound. Indeed anything

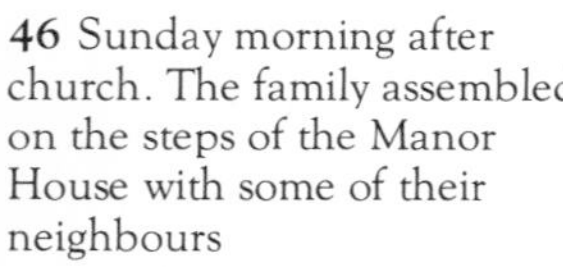

46 Sunday morning after church. The family assembled on the steps of the Manor House with some of their neighbours

so radical as a tax upon their incomes in peace-time seemed to the upper classes like the beginning of the end, although until the agricultural depression of the 1870s began to bite into their estates, the territorial grandees continued to enjoy the good things of life to which they had been accustomed, and if politics were their main preoccupation, sport was their favourite pursuit. The 14th Earl of Derby, leader of the Tory party and three times Prime Minister, accepted office merely as a duty, not from any motive of self aggrandizement or ambition. He was a clever man, a classical scholar and one of the finest orators of his generation when he cared to exercise his gifts; but Disraeli, as his henchman in the House of Commons, found him elusive and at times, maddening, since he remained deliberately unmoved by the dramatic element in politics and calmly conducted the business of the state from his Lancashire home when he was suffering from an attack of gout, or it did not particularly suit him to travel up to London.

Knowsley, the Earl's ancestral seat half way between Liverpool and Wigan, had been in the family since the Middle Ages and was one of the largest houses in the kingdom, each generation having added bits and pieces to it, including a gigantic dining-room in the Gothic style built by the 12th Earl, which was so hideously cold it had to be abandoned in the winter. Except for a superb Rembrandt and some Dutch seascapes, there were no treasures at Knowsley to be compared with Chatsworth or Woburn. But it was here that Lord Derby could indulge in the pleasures of a country gentleman among his horses and his dogs, becoming, according to Greville, a totally different person from the dignified figure who guided the destiny of the nation from the House of Lords. 'In London he is one of the great political leaders,'

47 A shooting party in Scotland, where the gentlemen, suitably clad in kilts and knicker-bockers, forgathered without their wives to enjoy the stag hunting and grouse shooting

Greville wrote, 'and here he is a lively rattling Sportsman, apparently devoted to racing and rabbit shooting, gay, boisterous, almost clownish in his manners and without a particle of refinement.... He is certainly the most natural character I ever saw, never seems to think of throwing a veil over any part of himself ... and it is this that makes him so comfortable as he is.'

The Earl never succeeded in winning the great race at Epsom founded by his ancestor, though he owned a large stud and a rich racing stable at Newmarket and frankly enjoyed the company of his trainer, his jockeys and his stable lads rather more than that of his Cabinet colleagues. Unlike Greville, who so often lamented his own addiction to horse racing and thought 'it degraded and stupified his understanding', Derby never allowed anything to interfere with his enthusiasm for the Turf and never missed an

48 The 14th Earl of Derby, Prime Minister and leader of the Tory Party in the House of Lords. He was the owner of Knowsley Hall, an estate that had been in the family since the Middle Ages, a keen sportsman and a classical scholar. F. R. Say

important meeting. As a leading member of the Jockey Club, he travelled from one race course to another, 'in high force and spirits, carrying everything before him', and when the two men met at York Races in the crisis year of the Crimean War, Greville noted sourly that 'not a word was ever uttered about politics.'

Not being a career politician, Derby did not care a fig what Greville or anyone else said or thought about him. He made use of Disraeli because it was necessary for the Tories to have a brilliant leader in the House of Commons, but there was a wide gulf between them in status and in sympathy and not all Disraeli's panache could gloss it over. He felt an outsider at Knowsley; horses did not interest him at all and unless the talk turned to politics he was bored. Yet as the self-styled 'defender' of English aristocratic

principles, Disraeli held a number of cards and even those who still thought of him as a charlatan and a pushing Jew could not do without him. Their condescension was sometimes galling, especially to anyone so highly strung, for whereas many Victorian gentlemen thought it bad form to show their feelings, Disraeli's oriental temperament made it impossible for him to conform to this stiff upper-lip, public school convention. He had, however, one great compensation in the unique personal relationship he enjoyed with the Queen when at last he achieved his ambition and became her Prime Minister.

49 Racing at Newmarket. The sporting aristocracy devoted much time and money to the breeding and training of racehorses and dominated the Turf through the Jockey Club

It was precisely his colourful, un-English qualities that made him so attractive to the middle-aged widow of Windsor. She disliked Mr Gladstone. All his zeal, his punctilious attention to ceremony and his high-minded principles went for nothing, since in spite of his wife's advice 'to pet her a little', he could not, or would not, unbend with the Queen. She complained that he always addressed her as if she were a public meeting, unlike his rival – '*dear* Mr Disraeli' – who understood her perfectly. He wooed her with exquisite flattery, capturing her heart and her imagination by appealing to the emotional side of her nature for so long suppressed by the gloom and frustration of her life without Albert. She became younger and prettier looking, those pouting lips in that round, obstinate face, smiling and chattering with a new gaiety that surpassed all ordinary intercourse between the Sovereign and her Prime Minister. He persuaded her to reappear in public, to open Parliament in person, to review the troops and distribute medals at Aldershot; and for six years in private audience with her, through all the ups and downs of political strife, he kept her enthralled.

Writing to a friend from Osborne, he said: 'I can only describe my reception by telling you that I really thought she was going to embrace me. She was wreathed with smiles and as she tattled, glided about the room like a bird.' Then he added significantly: 'We are never so pleased as when we please others and, in our gratified generosity, attribute to them the very results we have achieved.' Thus the elderly decaying Jew, with his gout and his asthma, his dyed curls and his yellow face, laid his far-flung achievements as a statesman at the feet of his 'Faery Queen', and by giving her reverence, romance and a rapturous sense of her own imperial majesty, enhanced the prestige of the monarchy in the eyes of the whole world. And thus by a strange irony which Disraeli himself enjoyed to the full, Victorian politics were dominated for a considerable period by the most alien and un-Victorian figure in Society, by the dandified, oriental nobody who had stormed the heights of the exclusive English aristocracy to become Prime Minister, Earl of Beaconsfield and the object of the Queen's undying affection. To no one else did she send bunches of primroses gathered by herself in the woods of Osborne with a little private note signed: 'Ever yours very aff'ly, V R I.'

Disraeli had always enjoyed the company of women and in consequence was never a very enthusiastic clubman. He did, however, recognize the significance of the Carlton Club as the social citadel of Toryism and after being proposed and seconded by Viscount Strangford and the Marquess of Chandos, he wrote jubilantly to his sister: 'I carried the Carlton. The opposition was not considerable in committee but my friends were firm – 400 other candidates and all in their opinion with equal claims.' It was a step up and a tremendous relief, for there was nothing more humiliating than to be blackballed and excluded from a London club and such a calamity was not easy to live down.

The clubs, as an English institution, had evolved out of the seventeenth- and eighteenth-century coffee houses around St James's Street, where gentlemen of rank and fashion had been in the habit of gathering to gossip, gamble and debate the political news of their time. In the days of the Regency, Beau Brummel and the dandies had monopolized the bow window at White's and Charles James Fox was to be found gambling at Brooks's without a break from 8 o'clock in the evening until 3 o'clock the next afternoon. But by the 1840s a number of new clubs had been established, where members could sit and read the newspapers in comfortable leather armchairs after dining off a mutton chop in the coffee-room, or instead of gambling hectically at hazard, faro and ombre, enjoy a modest game of whist in the card room.

St James's Street was too narrow and too congested for the palatial premises needed to house the United Service Club, the Athenaeum, the Travellers, the Reform and the Carlton, all of which were built after the

50 Benjamin Disraeli: the dandified, oriental nobody who stormed the heights of the exclusive English aristocracy to become Prime Minister, Earl of Beaconsfield and the object of the widowed Queen's deepest affection. Sir John Everett Millais R.A.

demolition of Carlton House on the 'sweet shady side' of Pall Mall within walking distance of the mansions in Mayfair, the government offices in Whitehall and the Houses of Parliament. No other situation could have been more convenient and no other institution gave the male sex quite the same facilities for social, political and intellectual intercourse — or such a splendid refuge from feminine interference, since no lady ever even thought of invading this exclusive masculine preserve and no female servants were employed except in a very junior capacity as under-housemaids confined to the basement and the backstairs. The hall porters, the coffee-room waiters, even the boy who marked up the scores in the billiard-room, were scrutinized by the committee for their honesty and good behaviour. And rules for the members were equally strict: no smoking allowed except in the billiard-room, no bad behaviour or drunkenness, no rudeness to the club servants and no guests permitted to penetrate beyond the front hall under threat of expulsion.

The United Service Club admitted no members under the rank of major in the army or commander in the navy and as most of the officers in the armed forces came from the highest aristocratic circles, it was very exclusive.

51 The United Service Club, Pall Mall, founded after the Battle of Waterloo for senior officers of the armed forces, all of whom belonged to upper-class families. W. Lee

Many of them, like the Duke of Wellington, were younger sons of the nobility and gentry, who had bought their commissions; and if their qualifications were not always so important as a means of advancement as their connections with the governing class, it was felt that the army was safer in their hands than if commanded by 'unprincipled military adventurers', who might well constitute 'a danger to the liberties of the nation.' High-ranking officers who survived the Crimea, the Indian Mutiny, the Ashanti and China Wars, returned to fight their battles all over again in the quiet coffee-room of Nash's beautiful club house and as professional soldiers, damned the politicians for their ineptitude and armchair strategy. Egocentric, choleric and accustomed to exercising authority over their subordinates, they belonged to a world of action totally different from that of the gentlemen who walked up the steps of the Athenaeum on the opposite side of Waterloo Place.

Sir Humphrey Davy and John Wilson Croker founded the Athenaeum in 1824 'for the association of individuals known for their scientific and literary attainments, artists of eminence in any class of the fine arts and noblemen and gentlemen distinguished as liberal patrons of science, literature and the

52 The Athenaeum Club, established in 1824 by Sir Humphrey Davy and John Wilson Croker for 'the association of individuals known for their scientific and literary attainments'. G. B. Moore

arts.' Its list of members included a large number of bishops and clerical dons, antiquarians and classical scholars, orientalists, archaeologists, Royal Academicians, eminent lawyers and men of science, successful authors and successful sculptors: men whose birth and breeding were of less importance in these august surroundings than their achievements. William Butterfield, a pioneer of the High Victorian Gothic style in architecture, was in the habit of walking round to the Athenaeum every afternoon 'to get his dish of tea and perhaps to hold conversation with those persons whose privilege it was to know him.' As the son of a small tradesman, apprenticed to a builder at the age of 14, before turning to the more socially acceptable career of an architect, he had climbed as high as he could get and was sensible of the honour conferred on him by his election to the Club. Tall, bespectacled, with long side whiskers and a balding head, always respectably dressed in a black frock-coat, a white linen shirt and a tall hat, he could have been mistaken for one of his upper-class patrons. Yet 'the privilege of knowing him' was largely a fiction of his first biographer, for Butterfield was a lonely man with an introspective nature and he never really succeeded in reaching any sort of intimacy with his fellow members at the Athenaeum.

Privacy evidently meant more to some clubmen than intimacy. At the Travellers, the splendid Italian palazzo built by Sir Charles Barry next to the Athenaeum, there was a Silence Room, which, even if it served to protect members from boring each other with long travellers' tales, was all the more extraordinary because the Club had been established originally as 'a point of reunion for gentlemen who had travelled abroad.' To qualify for membership it was necessary to have journeyed outside the British Isles for a distance of not less than 500 miles in a direct line from London, though this qualification by no means ensured the election of any particular candidate and among those who were blackballed were the ruthless, self-made adventurer Cecil Rhodes, the sporting Earl of Rosebery and Lord Lytton, the Viceroy of India.

Election to the Reform Club, next door to the Travellers, and to the Carlton farther along Pall Mall, depended on the political colour of the candidate. The Liberals at the Reform enjoyed the best food of any club in London when the famous French chef, Alexis Soyer, was employed there and created his celebrated *Côtelettes à la Reform* for the gastronomic delight of the members. At the Carlton, the Conservatives did less well and were continually complaining of the tough meat and high prices: 1s 6d for a cut off the joint and 1s for 'a second help', 6d for a tart, which according to one member, was 'less than a mouthful' and 3d for a portion of cream to go with it. The committee agreed that larger tarts should be supplied in the future, but they rebuked Sir William Fraser for having used 'threatening language' to the staff in the coffee-room over some asparagus, which was 'examined and tasted by the committee and found to be good.'

Complaints of another kind were lodged by the residents of Pall Mall against the Marlborough Club, founded by the Prince of Wales with the help of a backer, described as 'an old snob called Mackenzie, the son of an Aber-

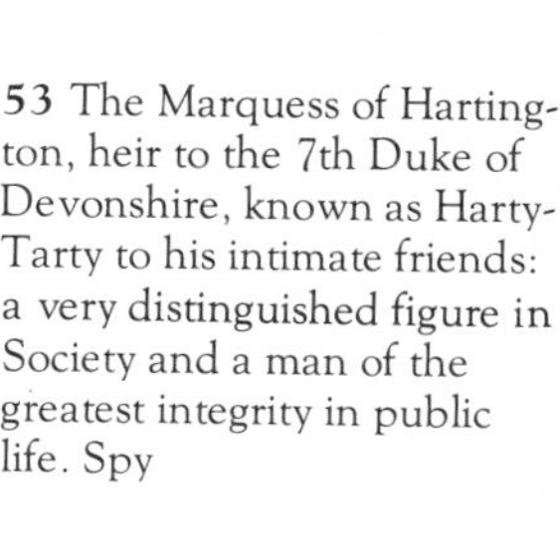

53 The Marquess of Hartington, heir to the 7th Duke of Devonshire, known as Harty-Tarty to his intimate friends: a very distinguished figure in Society and a man of the greatest integrity in public life. Spy

deenshire hatter who made a fortune in indigo and got a baronetcy.' Royal or not, the members of the club made such a racket in the bowling-alley on the premises it had to be roofed over and converted into a billiard-room before the worthy citizens of Pall Mall could get a good night's sleep. All the members were personally known to His Royal Highness and belonged to 'the fashionable bad set and betting people' of whom the Queen, not without reason, so strongly disapproved. One young man, Count Jaraczewski, familiarly known as 'Sherry and Whiskers', had to take a lethal dose of prussic acid rather than face arrest and ruin when the police caught up with him, and another member befriended by the Prince turned out to be an American swindler. These 'most inconvenient friends' as his mother called them, did not, however, deter the Prince, and the Marlborough Club was so close to Marlborough House he could walk over there in the evening for a game of baccarat without being seen.

Another member of the Marlborough Club to earn the Queen's displeasure, on account of his liaison with the beautiful Duchess of Manchester, was the Marquess of Hartington, but as he was heir to the 7th Duke of Devonshire and a very distinguished figure in Society, there was nothing much Her Majesty could do about it. The Prince called him 'Harty-Tarty' and was devoted to him, relying on his judgment as a man of integrity in public life and often invoking his assistance when his indiscretions got him into difficulty. For Hartington was above corruption and above personal ambition and although he was easily bored and apt to fall asleep at Cabinet meetings, he was never at a loss for the right answers to a problem and never known to have let a friend down.

He was a distinguished looking man with small hands and elegant feet and an unmistakable air of aristocratic dignity. Often described as a typical Victorian gentleman, he had a long nose, heavy-lidded eyes and a sensual mouth with a full lower lip accentuated by a reddish beard; but he was really far too complex a character to be typical of anything except his own individuality, which had grown out of the freedom his high birth had given him to pursue a way of life unhampered by any restrictions other than his own conscience. At the age of 28, already attached to the Duchess of Manchester, he surprised everyone by falling deeply in love with the prettiest of all the pretty horse-breakers of the *demi-monde* — Catherine Walters, otherwise known as 'Skittles' from the skittle-alley in a Liverpool public house where she had worked as a child for a penny a day.

Brilliant and beautiful with large violet-coloured eyes of a melting sweetness, a slender waist and sensitive hands, Skittles was a fearless equestrienne and when not riding in the Park, drove her black Orloff ponies with such panache all eyes were drawn towards her. Hartington was hypnotized and much to the chagrin of the Duchess of Manchester, he made no attempt to conceal his pleasure in the lovely young woman he escorted to the races and was seen with everywhere. He set her up in a small and elegant house in Mayfair — not as his friends would have done in a discreet villa in St John's Wood, where Catherine would have been hidden away under the

54 Catherine Walters, known as 'Skittles': the fascinating young woman of the *demi-monde* with whom the Marquess of Hartington fell passionately in love, setting her up in a small and elegant house in Mayfair

55 A West End night house. Victorian gentlemen often took their pleasure in the brothels around the Haymarket unbeknown to their wives and womenfolk

pretence of not existing at all; and gave her an income of £2000 a year, which she enjoyed from the Devonshire estate for the rest of her life.

Such generosity was rare among Victorian gentlemen and Hartington's lack of humbug was even more unusual. But he was far too realistic to think of Skittles as a future Duchess of Devonshire, and when the sudden blaze of publicity their affair engendered looked like destroying them both, he fled to America and stayed there until his emotions had cooled, returning eventually to England and to the Duchess of Manchester's drawing-room where he belonged. She gave him tea and enquired after his travels and they were soon on the old intimate footing that so distressed Queen Victoria but was accepted by the Duke of Manchester and everyone else. Indeed the affair was conducted with such decorum on all sides that Society was not in the least shocked until some 30 years later, when the Duke of Manchester died and Hartington, by then the 8th Duke of Devonshire, married the lady and took her to Chatsworth as his Duchess. Such fidelity was a bit of a joke among the Marlborough House Set.

Skittles, as the last of the great English courtesans, after a successful career in Paris and a serious love affair with the young and romantic Wilfred Blunt, retired to Chesterfield Street, where she gave elegant little tea parties on Sunday afternoons that were attended by a number of very distinguished Victorian gentlemen. Blunt had written his *Love Sonnets of Proteus* in praise of her as 'a woman most complete in all the ways of loving', and prodigal of love –

Brave as a falcon and as merciless ...
Untamed, unmated, high above the press.

But she also had a great capacity for friendship and her conquest of Mr Gladstone, when he called to ask her advice on the work he was doing to reform the London prostitutes, was a triumph.

Gladstone's nocturnal rambles in the streets were open to misinterpretation. It was not pleasure he sought when he stopped and spoke to the gaudy young women standing around the doorways of Mayfair, or only the pleasure of doing good; for it was his habit to persuade them to go home with him to Carlton House Terrace, where his charitable wife, Catherine, endeavoured to point out to them the error of their ways. Catherine never failed her husband in this awkward situation, though it cannot have been easy with a house full of respectable servants and with her own children asleep upstairs. Yet neither she nor anyone else ever thought that these unfortunate 'fallen doves', as they were called, might be less culpable than the gentlemen who pursued them in the streets.

Sex was regarded as an exclusively masculine prerogative. 'Nice' women had no pleasure in it. But the male animal had instincts and appetites that demanded satisfaction however deplorable and unseemly; and while it was sometimes embarrassing to be found out, Victorian gentlemen were at liberty to take their pleasure in the brothels in the Haymarket and to return home in silence to preside over the family breakfast table only a little the worse for wear. It was not their wives' business to enquire where they had been. It was not the thing to discuss such deviations from the straight and narrow path of respectability, or indeed to talk of sex at all. By a polite fiction Victorian ladies were supposed to be ignorant of the fact that prostitution existed and it was convenient for their husbands to keep up the pretence.

God created Adam and Eve and Eve gave Adam the apple to eat, so it could be argued that Adam was not guilty of original sin; and although Hippolyte Taine, a French visitor to London in 1872, was appalled by the numbers of prostitutes he saw soliciting in the streets with 'nothing brilliant, bold or smart' about them as in Paris, the English gentleman who furtively manoeuvred one of them into an arbour at Cremorne Gardens, was able to quiet his conscience and retain his self-esteem. He may even have thought that as the ladies of the town belonged to the 'lower orders', he was doing them a good turn.

6
The Ladies

The bride, the wife and mother, the widow and the grandmother — each phase of Victorian womanhood had its own status; and although there were frivolous and idle fashionable ladies who did not take their responsibilities very seriously, even they paid lip service to the duty required of them. For marriage was the first essential and motherhood the sacred function of the female species.

Almost any husband was better than none, better than the sad fate of the spinster, old at the age of 30, unwanted and incapable of fulfilling the natural purpose of her existence. Hence the anxieties, the fretfulness and the excitements that stirred in the bosom of the family when a young girl hovered between more than one suitor or set her heart on someone of whom her parents disapproved. She was not allowed, of course, to show her feelings too openly and it was a mistake for her to attempt to be too clever. Victorian men looked for virtue and simplicity in their wives, not for intelligence, for purity and a sentimental sweetness, not for boldness or independence; and if a betrothal was agreed between two young people, it did not mean that all their difficulties were over. The lawyers of both families took time to reach agreement over the complicated marriage settlements and nothing could be done before the parents gave their consent to the bargain.

'Blanche told Lord Airlie whenever you and he settled it she was ready,' Lady Stanley wrote to her husband. 'I think she is not as much amused with this part of the business as she wishes — she is very capricious and changeable and I shall be very glad when she is married.' Blanche, however, gave her fiancé a copy of Keble's book *The Christian Year* and they spent some happy hours reading it together under the trees of Alderley, and Airlie promised his bride a Scotch terrier, a deer-hound 'for the drawing-room', a mastiff and a retriever, 'and I suppose everything else she fancies,' her mother added. Meanwhile her trousseau was assembled and seen by Jane Carlyle when she visited Alderley shortly before the wedding in 1851. 'There was a fine rattling houseful of people,' she wrote. 'Lord Airlie was there and his sister and various other assistants at the marriage. And I saw a trousseau for the first time in my life, about as wonderful a piece of nonsense as the

Exhibition of all Nations. Good Heavens, how is any one woman to use up all those gowns and cloaks and fine clothes of every denomination? And the profusion of coronets! every stocking, every pocket-handkerchief, everything had a coronet on it! . . . Poor Blanche doesn't seem to know, amidst the excitement and rapture of the trousseau whether she loves the *man* or not,' Jane added. 'She *hopes* well enough for practical purposes.'

She certainly had no cause to complain of her wedding journey, for Airlie fulfilled her romantic dream 'of being carried to a castle at once.' After the wedding ceremony, he took her away in a new travelling carriage, leaving Alderley at 11.15 in the morning and arriving at Cortachy Castle, his home at the foot of the Grampians, at 3.00 a.m. the next morning. There were 'bonfires, cheers and torches all the way from Glamis . . . and I walked into my new home amidst the deafening shouts of a large crowd,' Blanche wrote excitedly. 'The Castle was illuminated. Airlie looked so happy and handsome, it was a perfect moment never to be forgotten and I hope neither he nor his people will ever regret my being here.'

Blanche was spared an interfering mother-in-law — the dowager Countess of Airlie had died some years before. Jennie Churchill as a bride was not so fortunate. Her arrival at Blenheim with Lord Randolph was greeted with similar demonstrations from the loyal people of Woodstock, who unhitched the horses from their carriage and pulled it through the park to the grand entrance of the palace, where the Duke and Duchess of Marlborough were waiting to great them. The Duke, though a proud and undemonstrative man, showed great courtesy towards his new daughter-in-law; the formidable Duchess did not succeed in concealing '*une certaine aigreur*' in her manner. She did, however, undertake the responsibility of introducing Jennie into Society, feeling that it was her duty to do so. At Blenheim this meant calling informally on some of the neighbours, but in London the ritual was far more complicated.

Indeed the whole business of paying calls and leaving cards, which occupied so much of a Society lady's time, was both tiresome and bewildering, besides being fraught with pitfalls for those who were unfamiliar with the etiquette the occasion demanded. Ceremonious calls, though known as 'morning calls', took place between 3 and 4 o'clock in the afternoon and lasted a quarter of an hour, no more and no less. They were entirely formal and signified the desire of one lady to pursue the acquaintance of another and if possible to get on to her guest list. Later in the afternoon, between 4 and 5 o'clock, calls were slightly less formal, and after 5 o'clock they were altogether more friendly, though even then they were not equivalent to an invitation to a tea-party, which required a basis of greater intimacy before it was given or accepted.

Calling was tied up with the still more esoteric politeness of leaving cards. The lady would sit outside in her carriage while her footman rang the front door-bell to enquire if the mistress of the house was at home. If the answer was 'no', she would give him three visiting-cards to hand in — one for herself and two for her husband. If the answer was 'yes', she would descend from her

56 The queue of aristocratic carriages in the Mall on a Drawing-Room day gave the common people some excitement. It was not the thing to do to draw the blinds down, though to be stared at was an ordeal for some of the young débutantes

carriage and after making the call, leave her three cards in the hall with the footman of the house. Any lady who failed from ignorance or absent-mindedness to observe these rules, committed a social solecism, or perhaps, was too ill-bred to realize the necessity of making the correct gesture towards the *grande dame* she wished so much to cultivate. If she was not already in the 'best Society', she would not venture to call at all, simply to leave a card announcing that she had arrived in town in the hope that the *grande dame* would condescend to leave a card on her in return to signify that the acquaintance might become a little closer.

The next step towards greater intimacy was an invitation to 5 o'clock tea, a gathering of ladies with perhaps an idle bachelor or two brought in to hand round the cups, the cucumber sandwiches, small cakes, 'sugar plums and cream or fruit ices of all Sorts', supplied to the nobility and gentry by the famous confectioner and pastry-cook, Mr Gunter of Berkeley Square. Sometimes the children of the household, both boys and girls dressed in frills and buckled shoes, came into the drawing-room at this time of day to be shown off to mama's guests and to recite a poem or sing a little song they had learnt by heart. French was spoken in front of the children so that these 'little pitchers with big ears' could not understand what their elders were saying, for gossip quite unfit for the young was the main topic of interest in this rather dead hour between luncheon and the more serious business of changing for dinner.

As a very vital, young American, eager for pleasure and excitement, it was not surprising if Jennie Churchill found the tea-parties and the cumbersome etiquette of calling and leaving cards somewhat frustrating. Brides were not supposed to go into Society too soon after their marriage and she created

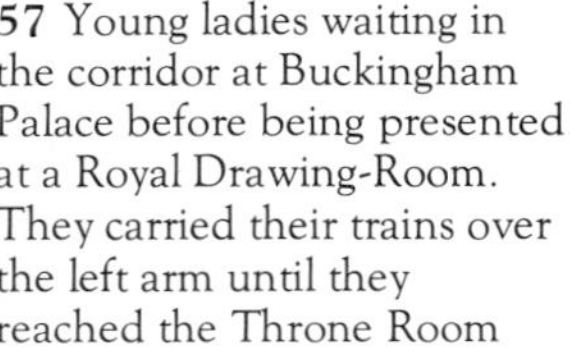

57 Young ladies waiting in the corridor at Buckingham Palace before being presented at a Royal Drawing-Room. They carried their trains over the left arm until they reached the Throne Room

quite a sensation by appearing at a ball attended by royalty before she had been presented at Court. Eyebrows were raised and quite a few of the aristocratic dowagers at the ball 'failed' to recognize her even with the aid of their lorgnettes, though their husbands were willing to forgive anyone so attractive for breaking the rules. And shortly afterwards her mother-in-law called for her in the Marlborough state coach at 2 o'clock in the afternoon to join the queue of carriages in the Mall on their way to the Royal Drawing-Room. 'The Duchess was very kind to me and lent me some rubies and diamonds which I wore in my hair, and my pearls on my neck,' Jennie wrote. 'And I also had a bouquet of gardenias she sent me.'

The Throne Room at Buckingham Palace was a splendid sight and the Prince of Wales, deputizing for his mother, looked very handsome in the full dress uniform of the Grenadier Guards. Among all the young ladies curtseying to him in a flurry of feathers, lace and tulle, Jennie's beautiful figure did not fail to catch his connoisseur's eye. He had, as he said, a particular fondness for American women: 'I like them because they are original and bring a little fresh air into Society. They are not so squeamish as their English sisters and they are better able to take care of themselves.' Jennie had all these virtues and very soon it was obvious to everyone that His Royal Highness liked her very much indeed. She was gay and witty. She dressed superbly, with a style and a simplicity that made other women look dowdy or overdecorated, and her first Season as a married woman could not have been more successful. When it came to an end she went off on a round of country house visits with her husband, arriving at Blenheim in time for the shooting season; and it was after an outing with the guns that she began to feel ill and was hurriedly accommodated in a very plain groundfloor room at

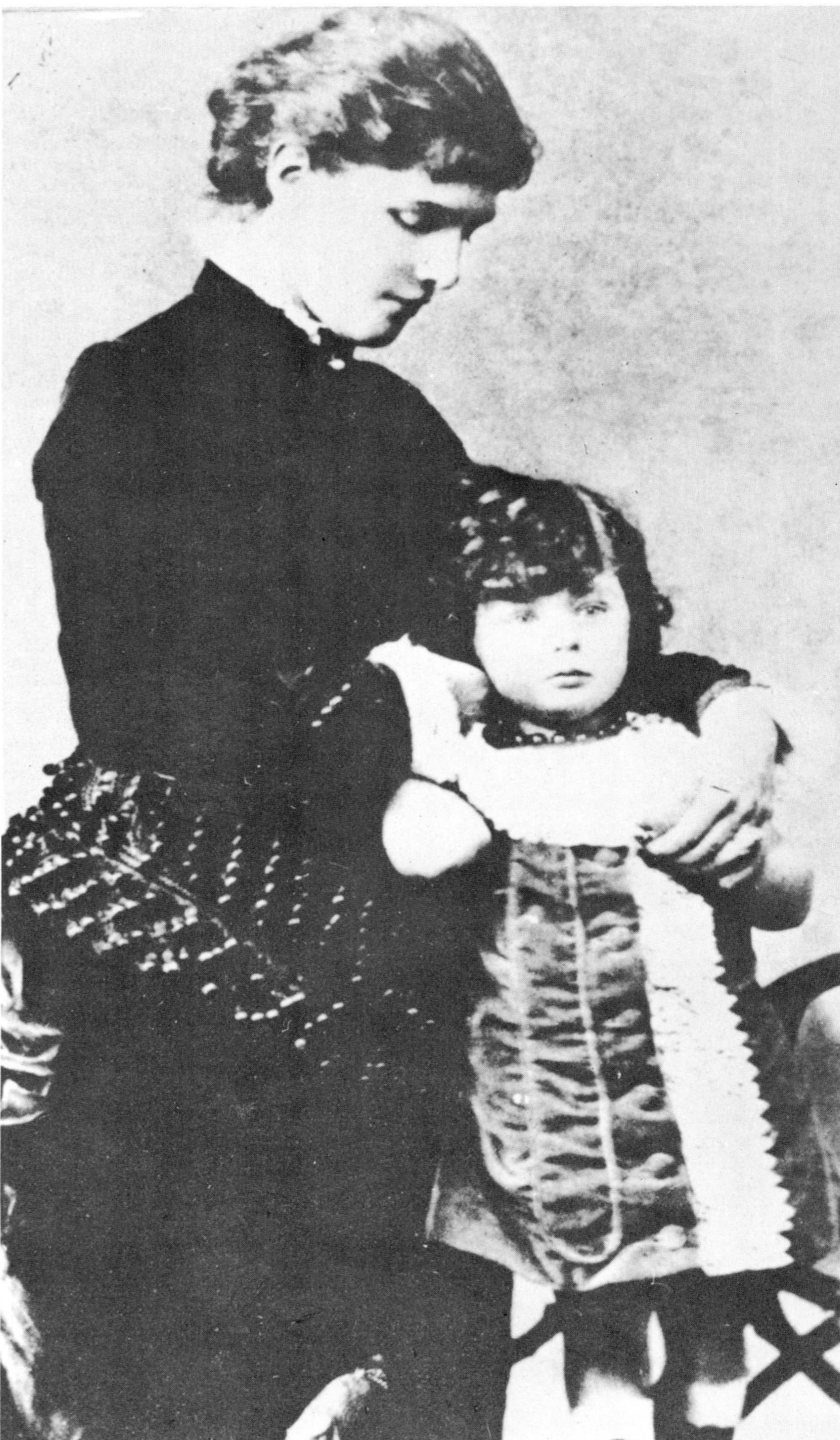

58 Jennie Churchill and her son Winston. His earliest memories of her were of 'a fairy princess from afar' kissing him goodnight

the palace, where she gave birth to her first child at 1.30 a.m. on 30 November, 1874.

Winston Churchill's earliest memories of his mother were of 'a fairy princess from afar' kissing him goodnight. 'She shone for me like an evening star,' he wrote. 'I loved her dearly — but at a distance.' It was his nurse, Mrs Everest, a wholesome, down-to-earth woman with an inexhaustible fund of patience and kindness, who looked after him and was his 'confidante'; for Jennie, busily pursuing the social round from one engagement to the next, was only too glad to accept the English upper-class convention of leaving her children in the nursery until they were old enough to go to school. No one thought there was anything wrong about this arrangement or that it showed any lack of affection. Nannies were faithful and reliable women and very dearly loved by the children in their care.

Yet motherhood was an absorbing preoccupation with the ladies of the nineteenth century not wholly devoted to the razzle-dazzle of fashionable Society, and large families of eight, ten or twelve children, even with nurses and nursery maids to look after them, were a great responsibility. Catherine Gladstone always seemed to find time for her children. With her remarkable energy and capacity for managing everyone around her, 'Pussy' as she was called, dominated her brothers and sisters at Hawarden Castle, the Glynne family seat on the Welsh border. Her charming bachelor brother, Sir Stephen Glynne, was quite happy to leave the estate in her capable hands and to welcome her husband into the family home, though Gladstone's father was a wealthy, self-made merchant in Liverpool and not of the established gentry. No doubts about marrying someone not absolutely out of the top drawer ever entered Catherine's own mind; she saw people as people, without the conventional overtones of snobbery that influenced most of her own class, and would embrace a poor, sick woman as readily as one of her own relations. And William Gladstone was a giant in her opinion, a prophet and a seer, a man superior to all his fellows, almost a saint, destined to carry the whole burden of England's future greatness. Never was there such a man, never would there be such another. Through almost 60 years of married life she never altered her opinion of her husband, nor did he ever have any reason to revise what he had written in his diary the day after their wedding, describing 'the brightness of my treasure, her pure enduring brightness.'

In the early days of their marriage William gave his wife the choice between knowing none of his political secrets or knowing them all and preserving absolute silence. She chose the second alternative and though careless, impetuous and indiscreet in many things, she never allowed a word to escape her lips. It was only when political business in London took him away from her that she complained bitterly. 'I feel so incomplete without you,' she wrote and again: 'Whenever you are away the sunshine seems gone.' She knew it was wrong and wicked of her not to have more courage and she deplored her own weakness, but thanked him profusely for the 'beautiful' letter he sent her, in which, at great length, he expounded the Christian duty of self-denial and obedience to the will of God, quoting Dante — *In la Sua volontate e nostra pace* — and concluding with a philosophical sermon that was a great comfort to her.

Her first child, William, was born in 1840, a fortnight before her sister, Mary Lyttelton, gave birth to a daughter. A second child, Agnes, was born two years later, a third in 1844, to be followed by two more boys and three more girls, one of whom died at the age of four. Catherine nursed all her babies in defiance of the prevailing custom of engaging a wet nurse to feed them and maintained a strict authority in the nursery. She sat up all night with the children whenever they were ill, dosing them somewhat impetuously with blue pills, grey powders and other concoctions of her own making, and they were some compensation for her loneliness when Gladstone was away from home. Willy, her first born, was her favourite: a sensitive little boy, inclined to be indolent in a household that was always bursting with activity. Agnes was beautiful, Stephen serious-minded like his father, and the little ones high-spirited, healthy and happy. Catherine gave them all their first lessons and insisted on hearing their prayers every night at bed-time; and as well as mothering her own family, she was deeply involved with her sister's boys and girls, with her younger brother's children and a horde of more distant relatives who came and went at Hawarden in droves.

It was not only in the bosom of her own family that 'Pussy' Gladstone worked for the comfort and joy of everyone around her. With unlimited generosity and an abundant energy that never failed, she flung herself into charitable works — not like so many Victorian ladies sitting on committees in their own drawing-rooms, but going out and about among the needy and the underprivileged around Hawarden and in London. During the cholera epidemic in 1866 she was to be seen in the wards of the London Hospital among the East End women and children, comforting the dying and clothing the survivors, before carrying them off to the free Convalescent Home she established at Woodford or back to Hawarden to be cared for by the coachman and his wife in a house in the grounds. As a fund raiser she was quite shameless. She once asked a rich friend for a donation of £1000 and when she received £500 in answer to her plea, promptly sent the cheque back, which upset the donor so much Catherine got her £1000 by return of post. Lame ducks, orphans, prostitutes, out of work mill-girls — almost any human being in distress could touch her heart and her pocket, and her charity was never given with the air of a lady bountiful condescending to be kind. She gave because she loved giving.

As a political hostess, after Gladstone became Prime Minister in 1868, she was less successful and rather haphazard. Guests sometimes arrived at Carlton House Terrace for dinner to find their hostess had forgotten all about them and although by then the youngest of her children had reached the age of 14, she put her family and her charitable work before her social obligations as the wife of the Prime Minister. Dull parties and dull people bored her and the guests she invited to her 'little Tuesday drums' were more often than not her personal friends and the people she thought would be interested in her three unmarried daughters rather than the Liberal supporters it was her duty to entertain. One of her nieces, Lucy Cavendish, wrote that 'Uncle William kicked at the notion of having regular Parliamentary Squashes' and that her Aunt's little drums were far pleasanter, but added that she was afraid 'many people have had their feelings lacerated.' Indeed there were times when Catherine seemed to take a delight in bringing together the most ill-assorted people and such unconventionality was frowned upon, though her exuberance and her charm often succeeded in smoothing the ruffled feathers of her guests. She had no patience at all with the etiquette of calling and leaving cards and when she failed in this punctilious game of tit-for-tat, could only plead to the ladies she had offended that she was otherwise occupied with her good works and in caring for her husband. She never missed any

59 Catherine, née Glynne, the loving and beloved wife of William Gladstone: a woman of remarkable energy, deeply involved in her husband's political career, devoted to her children and her charitable work among the poor

occasion when Gladstone was speaking in the House of Commons if she could help it, climbing the long staircase to the uncomfortable Ladies' Gallery, where a small patch of the brass railing for years afterwards shone brightly where it had been polished by the gentle friction of her gloved hand.

Not every mother was capable of creating such a harmonious atmosphere in her household as Catherine Gladstone. Mrs Nightingale, a fussy, energetic lady of good birth, frustrated by her amiable husband's lack of social ambition, had great hopes for her daughter, Florence, and was bitterly disappointed when that eagle among the domestic hens of her generation showed a disposition to take flight. Florence was tall and graceful with wonderful chestnut-coloured hair, prettier than her sister, Parthenope, and more intelligent. When they both came out in London Society, Florence

60 Florence Nightingale and her sister, Parthe, at Embley, the Nightingales' home in Hampshire. Florence reacted violently against the domestic tyranny of upper-class family life. W. White

quickly became popular at dinner parties and balls and the centre of attraction in a wide circle of friends and relations. She was surrounded by eager suitors and to Mrs Nightingale there seemed no reason why she should not marry very soon and marry very well. But neither was there any possible reason why at home in the Nightingales' comfortable house at Embley, not far from the Palmerstons' home at Broadlands, she should be so discontented and difficult. She had everything in the world a young lady of her class and station in life could want: plenty of money, plenty of friends and admirers, ample leisure for painting and drawing and doing her needlework and all the time in the world for the social and domestic duties her mother and sister found so absorbing. What Mrs Nightingale did not know was that God had spoken to Florence and called her to His service.

She was absolutely certain she had heard the voice of God. She recorded it in a private note on 7 February 1837, just before her seventeenth birthday. But God did not tell her what kind of service He expected of her and it was many years before she found out – years of inward pain and conflict that made her physically ill, more discontented than ever, a problem to herself and to her exasperated family. Life at Embley became intolerable. 'Why write, read or paint when nothing can come of it?' she cried. And who could enjoy being read to, when it was like 'lying on one's back and having liquid poured down one's throat?' In her private journal she set down the agony of her feelings: 'Oh, weary days! Oh, evenings that never seem to end – for how many years have I watched the drawing-room clock and thought it would never reach the ten! Women don't consider themselves as human beings at all. There is absolutely no God, no country, no duty to them at all, except family.... I have known a good deal of convents and everyone has talked of the petty grinding tyrannies supposed to be exercised there, but I know nothing like the petty grinding tyranny of a good English family. And the only alleviation is that the tyrannized submits with a heart full of affection.'

That was the trouble. Florence felt a filial duty towards her parents and gradually, as she began to believe that God had called her to the service of the sick, she was torn between what they demanded of her and what she knew she had to do. There were terrible family scenes. Parthe burst into tears, Mrs Nightingale had hysterics and her husband withdrew to his library, where he stood for hours on end at a high reading desk meditating on such abstruse subjects as the nature of moral impulses and the relation of ethics to aesthetics. Florence, in despair of ever persuading her mother to allow her to go abroad to train as a nurse, spent her time punishing herself for what seemed to be her 'sinfulness' or studying in secret the medical text books her family thought were unfit for feminine eyes. She refused her last and most attractive suitor, Richard Monckton Milnes who had pursued her for nine years, with some reluctance. 'I have an intellectual nature which requires satisfaction and that would find it in him,' she wrote, 'a passionate nature which requires satisfaction and would find it in him ... a moral, active nature which requires satisfaction and would *not* find it in his life.' Yet she still hesitated. If they could only combine their different powers in some great work, instead of 'making Society and arranging domestic things', perhaps she could find some satisfaction? No, it was no use! 'I know I could *not* bear his life,' she wrote desperately, 'that to be nailed to a continuation, an exaggeration of my present life would be intolerable to me — that voluntarily to put it out of my power ever to be able to seize the chance of forming for myself a true and rich life would seem to me like suicide.'

So the die was cast and there were more acrimonious scenes, the emotions of the Nightingale family having a way of exploding like Vesuvius in eruption, leaving everyone pale and exhausted and gasping for breath. Possessiveness, resentment and obstinacy inspired Mrs Nightingale to treat her daughter most cruelly. She could not and would not understand, and she was determined that Florence should not have her own ungrateful way. But God spoke again and made it clear to Florence that she must continue 'to dig for her little plan in silence'. At last, with the help of friends in high places, she managed to obtain some training as a nurse in Germany, so that by the time the Crimean War broke out she was sufficiently equipped to battle with the stench and the filfth and the horror of the hospital at Scutari and to bring some comfort into the lives of the wretchedly diseased and mutilated

61 Occupation at home. Early Victorian young ladies were not encouraged to use their brains, but music and the art of embroidery which could be practised under the watchful eye of mama, were desirable accomplishments

soldiers, who revered her as a saint. If she ever thought of the spacious and sweet-smelling drawing-room at Embley where her mother and sister still sat over their embroidery, chattering of trivial domestic matters, she had no regrets whatever.

Mrs Nightingale and Parthe, totally unaware of their own appalling hypocrisy, enjoyed the reflected glory that shone upon them when Florence returned to England in 1856, worn out with her work. 'I cannot believe she will live long,' Mrs Nightingale wrote. 'Long or short we bless God and are content that our darling has been permitted to do so much for Him and for mankind.' Yet both she and Parthe continued to harrass their darling unmercifully in the midst of the Herculean task she had set herself of reforming the deplorable sanitary conditions of the British Army at home and abroad. And when Mrs Nightingale was old and ill and out of her mind, Florence made the ultimate sacrifice of a dutiful daughter, returning home to take care of her. 'Oh, to be turned back to this petty, stagnant, stifling life at Embley,' she wrote in one of her private notes. 'I should hate myself (I *do* hate myself) but I should LOATHE myself, oh, my God, if I could *like it* and find "rest" in it!' There was no rest in it – and no release, either, until Mrs Nightingale died at last at the age of 92.

62 Boredom at home. The idle rich, upper-class ladies of leisure had too much time on their hands between luncheon and the hour of changing for dinner

But it was not only Florence Nightingale who suffered from the claustrophobia of Victorian family life. Daughters were utterly dependent, and brought up to believe in maternal authority. Mama knew best and had a habit of saying so on every possible occasion, or of assuming an aggrieved air of martyrdom if she was displeased. Mama must not be hurt or upset. She was often resting on the sofa before, or after, one of her many confinements, but her power over the household, disguised as maternal solicitude, permeated the stuffy drawing-room and extended into the servants' quarters behind the baize door; and as few Victorian matrons, unless they were ultra-fashionable, had anything outside their homes to occupy their time and energy, it was not surprising if some of them became autocratic and unyielding.

63 Mama and her daughters take tea in the garden. By the 1880s girls had learnt to play the exciting game of lawn tennis and enjoyed running about the courts

Their sons got off lightly. Their daughters were expected to submit and could do little else. Once they had left the school-room and were out in the world, they could do nothing and go nowhere without Mama or some reliable chaperone of whom Mama approved. It was only the American wife of George Darwin, writing in the 1880s, who thought the whole idea ridiculous: 'It seems to me unutterably vulgar that girls, who are well brought up, and sons, who are well brought up, should not be allowed to associate without every girl having her mother at her elbow to see that no indecency is committed.... The real truth is that the chaperones want the power in their own hands, and I believe, though they protest against it, they really enjoy the dances.'

Many young ladies plunged as quickly as possible into matrimony to escape the nervous stress of life at home and the watchful eye of Mama. Others, not so pretty or so marriageable, stayed in the family fold as unpaid companions to their ageing parents. There was nothing else for them to do. Society did not care about these Cinderellas and could find no other use for them. Two of the Dowager Lady Stanley's seven daughters were unmarried and lived with her at Holmwood after the death of her husband, but she was so dictatorial their lives were a nightmare. 'You cannot think what a sad house this is,' one of their nieces, Kate Stanley, wrote, 'not because the aunts are uneasy about Grmama but because they say she is wearing them out. Grmama finds faults with everything, most unjustly, accuses them of neglecting her and of worrying and not suiting her, and is as irritable and cross as any mortal can well be. She sees the doctor every day but he says there is nothing whatever the matter with her, but that she is old; he is much more required for the aunts who were both so scolded today, that Aunt Louisa went into hysterics and Aunt Rianette had palpitations – she says her heart is getting weaker and she is quite worn out.'

Lady Stanley, widowed at the age of 61, had, in fact, never become reconciled to leaving Alderley, where she had reigned as the mistress of a large house over a large family. She was fond of her son and her daughter-in-law, and the English law of inheritance that decreed the immediate removal of a widow from the home she had enjoyed with her husband for the whole of her married life, had to be accepted. But she was bored at Holmwood and her two daughters suffered in consequence. In her new house there were only 11 servants, and the cook she engaged decided at once that she could not 'take' to such a small establishment, 'with three ladies only and no practise in her art.' Entertaining at Alderley had been on a scale suited to the late Lord Stanley's importance in the county among his neighbours. Now his widow had moved to a new district and there was no one much to talk to and nothing much to do except find fault with everything, nothing, in fact, to occupy a mind so forceful as hers.

She did, however, spend hour upon hour writing letters in a clear, legible hand, expressing her vigorous and decisive views on a multitude of subjects to every member of the family, and she was far more indulgent to her grandchildren than to poor Aunt Louisa and Aunt Rianette. Surprisingly she did not interfere much with their upbringing, but when her eldest grandson, Henry, instead of seriously pursuing the diplomatic career designed for him, displeased his parents by wandering aimlessly about the Near East dressed as a Turk, she stood up for him. 'He is like a ship without a rudder or compass and nobody can tell what he may do next if not allowed to take his own way,' she told his mother. 'All you and Edward can do is to make him a proper allowance so as to give him no just cause for complaint and then leave him free to follow his own devices.' Such permissive advice did not unfortunately do Henry any good, but his grandmother died – at the age of 93 – before the horrid truth of his bigamous marriage to a Spanish woman of doubtful antecedents was revealed. Had she known her comments would have been less kind and Henry would have had some difficulty in explaining his behaviour.

Widows, like the Dowager Lady Stanley, endeavoured to keep some control over their families and were greatly respected. Following the example of the Queen, they denied themselves pleasure, continued to wear mourning and often turned to the Church in their grief. Osbert Sitwell remembered his paternal grandmother, Lady Louisa Sitwell, wearing black in the daytime and dark-hued green or brown in the evening, though her husband had been dead for 30 years, dying suddenly at the age of 42 only four years after their marriage and leaving her with two young children to

64 Dowager ladies took to a bath chair or a pony phaeton and like Queen Victoria herself, who never ceased mourning her dead husband, wore black silk and black bonnets for the rest of their lives

bring up. Doubts about the frivolity of worldly pleasures had already entered her head when, as a young woman, she wrote after a visit to the opera: 'The music was delicious, but I think – I think – this must be the last opera for me. I had a strong feeling that I ought not to be there and there were many things that shocked and offended me.... And the ballet! How anyone can like – or look at it, I cannot think.'

After her husband's untimely death when there could be no question of ever again enjoying such entertainment, Lady Louisa was occupied in restoring Renishaw to solvency before her son George came of age and being no fool, she succeeded brilliantly. She also became increasingly pious and devoted to good works, comforted by her faith and aided and abetted by her daughter, Florence, who grew up to become 'so much taken up with Heavenly things', she was looked upon as a saint. Mother and daughter, who settled at Gosden in Surrey after George's marriage, were surrounded by earnest Evangelical clergymen, and once a year travelled all the way to Keswick to attend a Low Church Convention in a tent rigged up for the purpose. There were special prayers and Bible readings, lectures on the Gospels and such subjects as 'the Lowering of Moral Tone by Fiction of the present day'; and in the midst of a terrible thunderstorm, Mr Webb-Peploe cried out 'Anywhere with Jesus!' and led the hymn singing in a sturdy baritone voice. It was all 'wonderful, beautiful and helpful' and seemed to Florence and her mother 'a little like Heaven'.

Back at home, Lady Louisa presided every morning over family prayers with grace and dignity. After breakfast the chairs in the dining-room were drawn back against the window and the butler withdrew, returning almost immediately to hold the door open as the other servants entered in single file strictly in order of precedence, eyes cast down and freshly laundered aprons put on after their excessive labours since the early hours of the morning. The females were carefully segregated from the males, who looked embarrassed, especially the insubordinate young footman, George, whose eyes showed 'a wild longing to escape'.

Young Osbert and his sister, Edith, felt a sneaking sympathy with the footman, but morning prayers at Gosden had to be endured before the day began. And nothing could have been more of a contrast than breakfast with their other grandparents, the Earl and Countess of Londesborough, who lived in great luxury. At The Lodge, their summer house at Scarborough, if the formidable Lady Londesborough with her 'white eagle's face' was in a good mood, she allowed her grandchildren to scramble round their elders for the peaches, nectarines, cold grouse, fish and eggs that loaded the sideboard and to amuse themselves with her two Pomeranian dogs, while the parrots and cockatoos she loved squawked in their cages hanging by the window.

A daughter of the 7th Duke of Beaufort and a cousin of the Duke of Wellington, Lady Londesborough was invariably far more benevolent towards her pets and her grandchildren than to the rest of her family. Even her extravagant, easy-going husband seemed to be a little afraid of her, while

65 The extravagant Earl and Countess of Londesborough (*4th and 3rd from the right* in the group under the lamp standard) entertain the Prince and Princess of Wales at a reception on the Spa at Scarborough in 1871. J. J. Barker

everyone else trembled before she spoke, her soft, and honeyed tone of voice masking the will power of a great lady who could not be trifled with and was a past master at snubbing anyone of whom she disapproved. She loved opera so passionately, she persuaded Lord Londesborough to take her to Egypt to hear the first performance of Verdi's *Aida* in Cairo, a trip that necessitated the marshalling of a very expensive retinue of servants, couriers, carriages, animals and baggage; and at Scarborough, which was then a fashionable spa, when she drove out in her carriage in the afternoon, people made way for her in deference to her rank. It was said that Lord Londesborough could ride for 60 miles or more without leaving his own ground in Yorkshire, his estate including whole towns like Selby, but when he died, his lavish spending left his heir in some difficulty and his widow had to retire to a smaller house, which she found intolerable. The brilliant life she had been used to slipped away through her long, aristocratic fingers. No one came to see her, no one trembled any longer when she spoke and she finished up in a bath chair, sadly discontented and alone.

Her daughter, Lady Ida, married Sir George Sitwell in 1882 when she was 17, and two more incompatible people could never have been joined together. Sir George was scholarly and lived in a peculiar dream world of the Middle Ages, his eccentricity aggravated by a highly sensitive nervous system which eventually turned him into a neurotic hypochondriac. Lady Ida was beautiful, with a small head poised on a long neck and exquisitely refined features. She was capricious, impulsive, sometimes cruel in a thoughtless way and wildly extravagant. She liked having people around her, seeking pleasure in their company and showering expensive presents on them. Domesticity baffled her and bored her, and she hated keeping accounts, since her meticulous husband invariably critized her helpless inability to add one sum to another correctly. She also disliked the pious religiosity of her mother-in-law, who in return found her frivolous and unreliable. But marriages in the Victorian era did not come apart, those who were joined together in church remained husband and wife, unless there were very exceptional circumstances.

Divorce was a dreadful calamity, especially for the wife. It made no difference whether she was innocent or guilty, whether her husband was a drunken brute or a rascal, she still ran the risk of being ostracized by Society, torn from her children and cast out to live the rest of her life abroad. No wonder that in such circumstances the ladies who grew tired of their own husbands and were sufficiently alluring to attract someone else's kept quiet. Provided they conducted their affairs with discretion as part of the social game, no one was very critical. It was taken for granted that young married women should have admirers, but Daisy Brooke broke the rules and caused an unprecedented scandal. Her spectacular marriage to the Earl of Warwick's heir in 1881 was apparently a love match. Lord Brooke was young and attractive, Daisy an heiress in her own right, who had been strictly brought up in the country. Marriage gave her freedom from parental control and she was suddenly thrown into the glamorous world of smart Society. Everyone was at her feet and Lord Brooke denied her nothing, content to go out shooting while she went hunting and learnt to drive a four-in-hand with great skill and daring. Her parties at Easton Lodge near Dunmow were gay, extravagant and brilliant. Nothing it seemed could go wrong. She had three children in quick succession and having thus done her duty to her husband's family, fell passionately in love with Lord Charles Beresford, a handsome, dashing young naval officer, married to a woman ten years older than himself.

No one was in the least shocked or scandalized until Daisy lost her head and the whole affair blazed up into the open. According to Lady Charles Beresford, Lady Brooke rushed into her boudoir one morning, declared her love for Lord Charles and her intention of eloping with him immediately and was utterly dismayed when Lady Charles refused point blank to allow such an insane project to go forward and ruin her husband's career. Lady Brooke vowed she would not give Lord Charles up and told the world she was the victim of Lady Charles's spite. But worse was to come. Some months later, when Lady Brooke was relaxing in the South of France, she heard that Lady Charles was expecting a child, which, as Lady Brooke noted, 'in view of her age, her ugliness and her pious character could only be her husband's.' Blind with fury she sat down and wrote an incriminating letter to her lover, which fell into Lady Charles's hands and was at once passed over to a solicitor named George Lewis, known to be an expert in dealing with the follies and transgressions of fashionable Society. George Lewis promptly informed Lady Brooke that she would find herself in serious trouble if she continued to annoy his client, whereupon Lady Brooke, casting around for influential assistance, thought of the Prince of Wales and flung herself at his feet.

His Royal Highness was appalled. Lord Charles was a close friend of his and the Prince had no doubt at all that the whole affair must be hushed up before any further damage was done. Yet here was a fascinating, irresistible damsel in distress, pleading with him to save her from social ostracism. 'He was charmingly courteous to me,' she wrote, 'and at length told me he hoped his friendship would make up in part, at least, for my sailor-lover's loss. He was more than kind ... and suddenly I saw him looking at me in a way all women understand. I knew I had won, so I asked him to tea.'

Lord Charles was sent abroad in command of a cruiser, ironically named *Undaunted*. Lady Charles, nursing her injured pride, asked the Prime

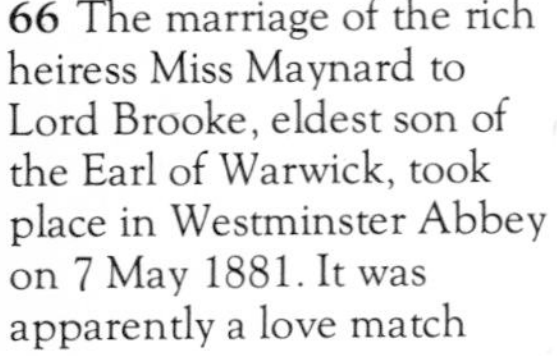

66 The marriage of the rich heiress Miss Maynard to Lord Brooke, eldest son of the Earl of Warwick, took place in Westminster Abbey on 7 May 1881. It was apparently a love match

67 'Daisy' Brooke, later Countess of Warwick. A keen follower of hounds, she caused a scandal by publicizing her love affair with Lord Charles Beresford but was rescued from her predicament by H.R.H. the Prince of Wales

Minister, Lord Salisbury, to intervene when His Royal Highness crossed her name off the guest list of a house party to which they had both been invited and put Lady Brooke's name down instead. Lord Brooke, behaving as an English gentleman should, said nothing at all. He remained convinced that 'a good day's fishing and shooting is second in point of pleasure to nothing on earth' and if his wife had other ways of fishing and shooting, that was no cause for a divorce or a separation that would involve the ageing heir to the throne and everyone else in yet another scandal.

Moreover it was only a year or two before His Royal Highness got tired of his darling Daisy. When she developed a startling enthusiasm for socialism and began to lecture him on the subject, he found her tiresome and rather ridiculous. He had been lectured enough long ago by his father and his mother was still doing it, and, anyway, socialism was vulgar and discreditable. A woman should not bother her head with such things. He wanted rest and refreshment, gaiety and charm, not a didactic female going on about politics and poverty, so he transferred his affections to the wife of George Keppel, who was very charming, very beautiful and very discreet.

7
The Young People

Babies in what she called 'the frog stage' did not appeal to Queen Victoria at all. While she often indulged in a mawkish sentimentality about people and things and sobbed herself to sleep when Prince Albert's favourite wolf hound died, she had a distinctly ambivalent attitude towards her children and very little patience with them when they were young. She resented the long and tedious business of pregnancy and was frightened of it, and when her nerves were 'horribly shaken', even her beloved Albert, because he was a man and exempt from her suffering, seemed not to understand how she felt.

They quarrelled violently over the little Princess Royal when, from a bouncing, healthy baby, she suddenly grew pale and sickly and did not respond to the treatment of the Queen's doctor, Sir James Clark. Albert, who was devoted to the child, thought Clark was at fault and the Queen's faith in him ridiculous. In a rage, he wrote a sharp note to her, declaring: 'Dr Clark has mismanaged the child and poisoned her with calomel and you have starved her. I shall have nothing more to do with it; take the child away and do as you like and if she dies you will have it on your conscience.' The Queen was equally furious and would not give way, until Baron Stockmar was hastily called in to pour oil on the turbulent dispute.

By then the Queen had to admit that the royal nursery was not running smoothly. Mrs Southey, a lady recommended by the Archbishop of Canterbury, proved to be incapable of exercising the proper authority. 'The nurses and nurserymaids are vulgar and from having no real hand above them constantly quarrelling,' the Queen wrote, while Mrs Southey herself complained that she felt she had lost the royal confidence and said she would be only too glad to relinquish her task as 'no bird can return more eagerly to her nest than I to my own home.' Again Stockmar was called in to solve the problem and after one of his lengthy memoranda setting out in detail the need for 'harmony and union' in the nursery, went on to enumerate the qualities required for the Royal Governess. She must be 'good and intelligent, experienced in the treatment of children, of good and refined manners, conciliatory and at the same time firm of purpose'; in short a person of unexceptionable character and 'a person of rank', since only a well-bred lady could maintain the necessary authority and 'her proper place towards the parents and the children.' Stockmar already had the Dowager Lady Lyttelton in mind, but was far too clever to do more than suggest her name to the Queen in such a way that the Queen believed she had thought of it herself.

In the event Sarah Lyttelton proved to be an ideal choice. She had all the qualities recommended by Stockmar, combined with a sense of humour and great kindness. Appointed in April 1842, six months after the birth of the Prince of Wales, she supervized the royal nursery for eight years until her health began to fail and the Queen reluctantly had to part with her. She was given absolute authority over the nurses and nurserymaids, had a footman to wait on her, and was 'so agreeable and sensible', that both the Queen and Prince Albert had complete confidence in her. A new head nurse, Mrs Sly, was engaged to replace the unsatisfactory Mrs Roberts, and the children immediately regained their health and spirits. They had been 'overwatched and overdoctored', Lady Lyttelton thought, besides being overdressed. At the age of two, the little Princess Royal was dolled up in 'Garter blue velvet, Brussels lace, white shoes, pearls and diamonds', until Lady Lyttelton persuaded the Queen to let her wear coarse straw hats and brown Holland frocks and blouses, except on very special occasions.

Both children adored their new governess and called her Laddle. The Princess Royal was very precocious and very naughty, but Lady Lyttelton did not think it was the child's fault if she sometimes cried when she was put on

68 The Queen and Prince Albert with their children at Osborne shortly after the birth of their ninth and last child, Princess Beatrice. They enjoyed the simple domesticity of family life. L. Caldesi

show. 'I do wish,' she wrote, 'that all her fattest and biggest and most forbidding looking relations, some with bald heads, some with black bushy eyebrows, some with staring, distorted, short-sighted eyes, did not always come to see her all at once and make her naughty.... Poor little body! She is always expected to be good and sensible!' And it made things very difficult for her governess when the Duke of Cambridge told the Queen that his own daughters '*never did* cry!'

The Prince of Wales was not an easy child, either. At times he was 'passionate and determined enough for an autocrat', but he still had 'his lovely mildness of expression and calmness of temper in the intervals' and was very sweet to his sisters, the Queen having given birth to another daughter in 1843 to add to Sarah Lyttelton's responsibilities. As the children grew up she gave them their first lessons, until Miss Hildyard was engaged to teach the Princess Royal and Mr Birch to tutor the Prince of Wales; and if she sometimes complained of her professional duties — 'accounts, tradesmen's letters, maids' quarrels, bad fitting frocks, desirability of rhubarb and magnesia and by way of intellectual pursuits, false French genders and elements of the multiplication table' — she was utterly devoted to the Queen's ever increasing family, and exercised a sane influence over the children which they were never to forget.

The royal nursery was modelled on the traditional upper-class concept of segregating young children from their parents until they were old enough to behave as adults, though in other houses, of course, the nursery was not

69 Children out with their nurse in the Shropshire countryside, the youngest wheeled out in a smart baby carriage, the eldest hoisted onto the back of a good-natured pony

supervised by a titled lady. It was the kingdom of the head nurse, or nanny, usually given the courtesy title of 'Mrs', like the housekeeper and the cook, but enjoying a unique position in the household. More a devoted friend of the family than a servant, nannies knew their place and what was due to them; and if they sometimes quarrelled with the other servants, it was nearly always to protect the children in their care and to defend their rights.

Lord Curzon of Keddleston had a savage nanny. 'She persecuted and beat us in a most cruel way and established over us a system of terrorism so complete that not one of us ever mustered up the courage to walk upstairs and tell our father and mother,' he wrote years later, remembering how she had tied him to a chair and locked him in a dark cupboard for hours on end, besides beating him continuously and forcing him to eat up the cold rice pudding he had left from the day before. But this fiendish woman was an exception. With all their quirks and old wives' tales, nannies on the whole were comfortable women with big bosoms to cry on and ample laps to sit in. They wore black straw bonnets, long stuff gowns in dark grey or black and large white aprons, and they gave the children in their care a sense of security, taught them good manners and respect and looked after all their needs.

Many of them were country girls, beginning as very young nurserymaids in the family and being handed down as they became more experienced from mother to daughter. Osbert Sitwell's nanny, Davis, had started as a nurserymaid with the Countess of Londesborough and having looked after Lady Ida as a child, became head nurse to her children, Edith, Osbert and Sacheverell. She was a gentle, placid woman, who possessed an instinctive understanding of young people and her life was dedicated to the Sitwell children. She doctored them when they were ill, punished them when they were naughty and at Scarborough, when their father's back was turned, bought them little paper bags of shrimps as a treat for their tea.

Young Osbert depended on Davis for everything and, like Winston Churchill, was only aware of his mother as a vision of beauty kissing him good-night, the scent of the tuberoses she always wore tucked into the corsage of her evening dress lingering in the night nursery to dispel his fear of the dark. Sometimes, although strictly forbidden to do so by Sir George, she brought him a peach or a strawberry ice from the dinner table and stayed talking to him; or in the daytime, when he and Davis, Edith and the baby Sacheverell were picnicking by the lake at Renishaw, she would suddenly arrive with a host of elegantly dressed and voluble friends, followed by a footman carrying rugs and cushions and parasols. For a moment she would join spontaneously in her children's pleasure, ignoring her adult friends and casting a radiance about her that filled young Osbert with delight. Then she would shiver with cold or become restless and bored, leading everyone back to the house and leaving the children and their nurse to follow more slowly.

It was a shock to Osbert to discover that his beloved sister, Edith, did not share his adoration of their mother. She was five years older than her brother: a sensitive, lanky young girl with straight fair hair and the long

Plantagenet nose of her Sitwell ancestors. Her lack of conventional beauty and her strange introspective temperament seemed to infuriate her mother, who constantly found fault with her in front of other people, driving her still deeper into a private world of her own. She liked music and poetry and was belittled in consequence; and though she had rather more in common with her eccentric father than her fashionable mother, with neither of them was she ever at her ease and she remained a bewildered victim of the conventional upper-class conception of what was good for children and what was not.

In the drawing-room, when they were dressed up and put on show, the children were expected to behave in a rational manner before an adult audience and to conform to their parents' tastes. In the nursery they had

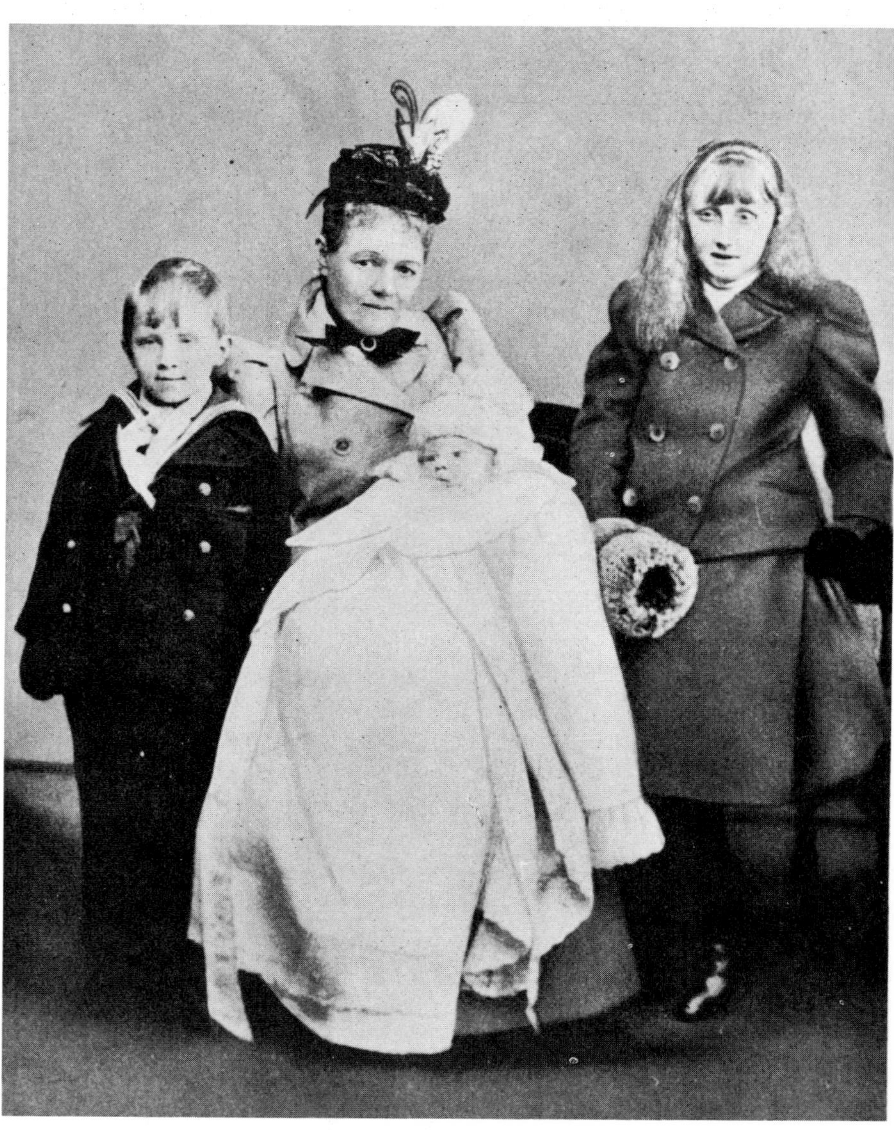

70 Mrs Davis, head nurse in the Sitwell household, with Edith, Osbert and Sacheverell in 1898. She was a gentle, placid woman who devoted her life to the welfare of the Sitwell children

more freedom. Brothers and sisters learnt to live with each other, the boys and the girls romping together and sharing their toys. Their diet was dull, with too much boiled mutton and too much rice pudding, and there were too many Gregory powders and other hateful nostrums in the nursery medicine cupboard, but their games were varied and exciting. They had rocking-horses, dolls' houses, jig-saw puzzles, toy theatres, table dioramas, stereo-scopes and magic lanterns to divert and instruct them. And the closed-in life of the nursery gave an extra thrill to the expeditions outside it. There were visits to the London Zoo and Madame Tussaud's waxworks, picnics in the summer and holidays at the seaside, and at Christmas, the huge family gathering of grandparents, aunts, uncles and young cousins, with a profusion of presents, tinsel stars, glittering candles, crackers and flaming plum-

71 Osbert Sitwell at the age of 3. Little boys wore sailor suits as soon as they were out of petticoats

pudding, and best of all, a never-to-be-forgotten outing to the pantomime at Drury Lane.

For the Victorian child a visit to the pantomime was an occasion of sheer magic that only came once a year. Osbert Sitwell remembered driving through the foggy, gas-lit streets in the Londesborough's carriage and arriving at the vast theatre in such a state of excitement that his nose began to bleed and he was made to lie down at the back of the box with a key down his back. He recovered sufficiently to be entranced by the brilliant spectacle on the stage when the great red velvet curtain rose on a demon-haunted wood with a fabulous fairy palace in the background and the Demon King met the Fairy Queen in a blaze of thunder and lightning. The dazzling costumes, the comical dame and the Prince Charming, so dashing in her short tunic, tight fleshings and high-heeled shoes, were all spell-binding; and the Transformation Scene, when curtains glittering with tinselled jewels rose and fell and dissolved into 'the silver Cascade of the Lily Bell Fairies in the Land of the Cloudless Skies', was a blissful and beautiful dream. Such things as rice pudding and Gregory powders were totally forgotten in this heaven of delight, where virtue always overcame wickedness in the end and everyone lived happily ever after.

72 Children, dressed in their best clothes and with their hair carefully brushed and curled, were put on show in the drawing-room and expected to behave in a rational manner before their elders. George du Maurier

73 'Our little brother'. Boys and girls grew up together in the nursery and a new arrival in the family was much admired

Quite a few children were encouraged by their parents to get up their own pantomimes and plays, to act charades and put on fancy dress. But life became harder for them when they left the nursery for the schoolroom. Governesses were harsher women than nannies — they had every reason to be. They came from the unhappiest class of Victorian society, inhibited by the miseries and frustrations of genteel poverty, and were often the daughters of impecunious clergymen or of some other respectable household that had come down in the world. Having failed to find husbands, they had no option but to go out as governesses, since any other kind of paid occupation was considered unfit for them. Whether they had the patience to deal with children or the gift of teaching them was immaterial; they went into bondage because they had to, and for many of them life became a penance. They suffered from nerves and indigestion, from the exasperating behaviour of their pupils and the capriciousness of their employers. Parents more often than not regarded them as a necessary evil and did nothing to alleviate their equivocal position in the household. They were not among the servants and did not sit or dine with the family — a tray was sent up to the schoolroom; and as one unfortunate individual wrote: 'The constant sense that a governess is deemed inferior in position is sometimes more than a sensitive mind can endure.'

Governesses from abroad suffered less from the in-built inferiority complex of their English sisters and were less neurotic. Lord and Lady Ribblesdale employed a gentle young woman from Alsace to teach their children, and as 'Zellie', a diminutive of the more stand-offish 'Mademoiselle', she quickly endeared herself to the whole family. She taught the children French from a tattered old book called *Le Livre de Madame Naslin* and the fables of La Fontaine and went everywhere with them, learning to live the English way of life in their uncle's superb country house at Gisburne, where Lady Ribblesdale's sisters, Margot and Laura Tennant, were frequent visitors and Tommy and Barbara went out hunting on their ponies. Discipline in the schoolroom was never very harsh in this lively and intelligent household. The children were encouraged to enjoy themselves and as they grew older, to

74 *Opposite, above* Magic Lantern shows in the drawing-room were an exciting novelty and entertained the whole family. The images were thrown on to a wide screen and by clever manipulation of the slides, appeared to move

75 *Opposite, below* Children of all ages were taken by their parents and grandparents to the Christmas pantomime as a great treat. Phiz

76 The pantomime at Drury Lane was a haven of delight for the young people who crowded the auditorium and watched with eagerness the magical transformation scenes

mix freely with their aunts and uncles and cousins and the eminent guests who filled the house from Saturday to Monday.

In due course Tommy was sent to Eton, but was spared the horrors of a prep school, unlike young Winston Churchill, who, at the age of eight, was sent to an establishment called St George's. In later life he described it as 'penal servitude', for the headmaster, Mr Sneyd-Kinnersley, systematically flogged the boys until they were almost dead with pain, and it was only Winston's faithful nurse, Mrs Everest, who, seeing the weals on his buttocks, courageously went to his mother and demanded that he should be removed forthwith from this appalling penitentiary. Winston never forgot what Everest had done for him and he never forgave his mother and the Duchess of Marlborough when they dismissed her in 1893. He was at Sandhurst at the time and wrote a passionate letter to his mother: 'She is an old woman – who has been your devoted servant for 20 years. She is more fond of Jack and I than of any other people in the world, so to be packed off in the way the Duchess suggests would possibly, if not probably, break her down altogether. Look too at the manner in which it would be done. She is sent away – nominally for a holiday as there is no room for her at Grosvenor Square. Then her board wages are refused her – quite an unusual thing. Finally she is to be given her congé by letter – without having properly made up her mind where to go or what to do.' Apparently the Churchills did not

77 Bible studies were taken very seriously in the schoolroom

even intend to provide Everest with a pension, which so incensed Winston, he sent her money from his own account at Cox's Bank whenever he could; and two years later when she was dying, he rushed up from Aldershot to sit by her bed until she became unconscious and 'her loving life of service to others' was over.

Winston's prep school experience was by no means unique. Almost anyone could set up a school for boys and many upper-class parents seemed to be quite oblivious of what they were doing in packing their sons off to these dubious reformatories. Lady Charlotte Guest sent her eldest son, Ivor, to a prep school at Mitcham run by a clerical gentleman, but it was not a success. She was so shocked by what Ivor told her about the swearing that went on, not only among the boys but from the headmaster himself, that she decided 'not to let Ivor go on exposed to such bad influences and so surrounded by temptations.' She drove over to Harrow in her open carriage to ask Dr Vaughan's advice about what to do with the boy before he could take up his place there and travelled from Leatherhead to the Isle of Wight and Winchester, looking at various schools before she finally found one at Totteridge which seemed suitable.

Ivor went to Harrow in 1850 and to his mother's delight was placed 'as high as it is possible for anyone to be on first entry', though she thought his quarters looked rather stark and miserable and she was worried to hear that

78 The cricket field at Harrow School in 1890. To be chosen to play in the 1st XI was to achieve the highest distinction. Edmund Evans

he was again 'a good deal tormented because he would not countenance the swearing which is so rife.' He looked 'pale and thoughtful' when she drove down to see him and evidently found the strain of remaining pure very exhausing. But Speech Days were a great occasion and his mother said the cricket field was 'a very pretty sight' on a summer afternoon.

Lady Charlotte had a great admiration for the celebrated Dr Vaughan. Lord Stanley of Alderley thought he was a prig and a fool. His second son, Johnny, a very lively, high-spirited boy of 14, had got into trouble at Harrow and was in danger of being expelled. The enormity of his crime apparently consisted in being up all night and in jumping over the dinner table in front of Dr Vaughan, a somewhat trivial breach of discipline which hardly seemed to warrant such drastic action on the part of the headmaster. 'It seems to me that there is much pettiness and littleness about Harrow,' Lord Stanley wrote in a letter to his wife. 'This minute interference with the boys, and espionage, is but a low mode of proceeding, and these followers of Dr Arnold who clothe themselves in lion's skin look more like other animals than lions.' At the same time if Johnny was taken away from Harrow, which Lord Stanley believed was preferable to having him expelled, he must be made to understand that he had misbehaved badly. 'If he won't work,' his father added, 'he must be shut up in his own room and deprived of his dog and not allowed to go out shooting without permission.'

But Johnny was not in disgrace for very long. After much deliberation the Stanleys decided to send him to Sandhurst, where in spite of 'the drunkenness and low habits practised there', he was perfectly happy and did very well. When he came home on leave he was very merry, and enjoyed 'lying on his bed with his dog and a French novel' and in 1854 he was promoted to the rank of Captain in the Grenadier Guards. He was dreadfully upset when bad health delayed his departure for the Crimea, as all his friends were going off to the war without him. But he got off at last, looking, his mother thought, 'very small to fight' and went into action with his regiment soon after he arrived at Sebastopol in June 1855. 'He has a right good heart in his slight body and we are all very fond of him,' his Colonel wrote, 'but he ought not to have been sent out at sixteen to rough it here, he has not the stamina for it.' And after a month in camp, tormented by the heat and the flies, he became so ill with dysentery, he had to be sent home, which he did not like at all. He had lost all his good looks and resembled 'a sick girl of eleven or twelve years old.'

Johnny's delicate health continued to cause great anxiety, but he recovered his looks and his gaiety and in 1858 was sent to India as ADC to the Governor General, Lord Canning. Though he never cared much for Canning, whose reserved and taciturn manner put a great strain on his staff, he immediately fell for Lady Canning, a woman of great charm and sensitivity, who had no children of her own and was delighted to have 'little Johnny' around. 'He is like a merry page,' she wrote, 'so civil and useful'; and again to his mother: 'Johnny's spirits never flag as you may easily believe and he enlivens our little party more than I can say and seems to be most easily amused. I believe nothing makes him happier than to talk about you and his sisters and you all seem to be always in his thoughts. I never saw a more affectionate creature.'

The young ADC's duties were not very arduous, though India was still seething with unrest after the blood shed of the Mutiny. He attended Lord Canning in the morning when he was occupied with government business, drove out with Lady Canning in the cool of the evening and made himself agreeable to the ladies at dinner. But Government House had all the snobberies and pettinesses of a confined circle. Mrs Stuart, the wife of the military secretary, was a tiresome, domineering kind of woman, 'who fancies one is there to wait on her,' Johnny wrote, 'and lays herself out to please in that peculiar manner one might called toadying.' Perhaps she knew he made fun of her behind her back with the other ADC, Major Bowie. She was certainly jealous of his devotion to Lady Canning and when he accompanied both ladies to the hill station at Coonoor, he wrote that 'Mrs S. is getting more grumpy than ever when I show my preference for Lady Canning. Of course I like walking with her, she walks like a goat, while Mrs S. puffs and blows and requires lifting over stones 1ft. high.'

Johnny had two bearers to dress him and take care of his things, 'one tailor and one washer-maid', a syce or groom for each of his horses and 'a grass-cutter', and he boasted gaily of 'roughing it' with Bowie at 'a most charming little breakfast, 20 servants looking on and 6 entrées.' But an ADC's pay was only £30 a month and good horses were expensive at 1600 rupees each, so Johnny was often in difficulties and as Lord Canning did not like him wearing a red waistcoat, he had to order a black embroidered one instead, which cost him £28 10s. He did not like India or the Indians very much. 'The longer I am out of England the more I love it,' he declared, 'and I certainly will never allow any woman in the world can compare (any more than other soldiers to Grenadiers) to an Englishwoman. I have seen what they consider the handsomest natives (nautch girls) and they never seem to have the slightest reflection of a soul in their faces or expression.' When, however, the time came for him to leave India, he realized 'what an enormous blank it will make in my insignificant existence not having Lady Canning to speak to and to look at'; and the night before he left Calcutta, when he went to say good-bye, he took her a little gold cross he had bought and asked her if she would put a bit of her hair in it for him to keep as a remembrance. Too overcome with emotion to wait for her answer, he kissed her hand and ran away, and half an hour later she sent the cross back to him with a lock of her hair enshrined in it and a little note wishing him God speed.

Johnny Stanley never saw his dear Lady Canning again. A year later, when she also was due to return home, she caught jungle fever and died tragically after a few days' illness, and by then Johnny was in Canada with his regiment and again very homesick for England. He loved Alderley and had a great effection for all his brothers and sisters. He was more tolerant than the rest of the family of his elder brother, Henry, who continued to rove around the East dressed as a Turk, and was on very good terms with his younger brothers,

Lyulph and Algernon. Lyulph was the most brilliant member of the family. He went to Eton in 1851 and then to Balliol College, Oxford, where the famous Dr Jowett thought very highly of him and said: 'There is so much go in him, I am sure he will do well.' He took a first class honours degree and became a Fellow of Balliol, yet the great promise he showed was never quite fulfilled, perhaps because he adopted very Radical opinions and as a strong supporter of John Bright gave offence to a number of people in high places. 'It is difficult I know for those who have been brought up in certain ideas suddenly to change,' he told his mother with typical youthful arrogance, 'but until the upper classes do change you must not complain if such as Bright accuse you of selfishness and spoiling the people.'

Lyulph was particularly incensed by the idea that the family living at Alderley should be earmarked for his brother, Algernon. To him it seemed abominable that 'the spiritual welfare of thousands should be made over to bolster up the finances of a younger son', especially as Algernon showed no real vocation for the Church. At Harrow he was idle and lazy and made no attempt to learn anything at all. In fact he was more of a problem to Lady Stanley than Johnny had been and in 1858 she wrote to her mother-in-law: 'We have made a great decision about Algernon. We are going to move him from Harrow to Rugby. He is doing no good where he is, and the choice lies between a private tutor and Rugby and the latter gives him a chance of strengthening his character in a rough sphere where more coercive measures are used. Perhaps you will think Rugby is not gentlemanlike — it is not polished, but anything is better for Algernon that will change the sauntering, idle, lazy tone of his mind and manner.' This purpose was achieved. Algernon's conduct improved under the rigorous discipline of Rugby, but he never obtained the living at Alderley because his father disliked his leanings towards Anglo-Catholicism, and in due time, to the shocked amazement of the whole family, he went over to the Church of Rome and settled in Italy.

Some boys enjoyed their schooldays in spite of the bullying, the flogging, the bad language and the spartan life they were forced into. All the eight Lyttelton boys went to Eton and except for Alfred, who hurt his back, were enthusiastic cricketers like their father, each in turn getting into the first Eleven. This meant they were looked upon as giants and treated with great respect by their schoolfellows, unlike Lord Robert Cecil, who found Eton in the 1840s intolerable. A frail little boy of outstanding intelligence, he wrote such brilliant essays, the bigger and stronger boys tormented him horribly, trying to force him to do their homework. When he stood out and refused, they pinched him and kicked him and pulled his hair, until his health and work were affected. He grew to hate Eton so much that his obstinate father was at last persuaded to take him away and to engage a tutor at Hatfield instead. Years later, as 3rd Marquess of Salisbury, he sent his own sons to Eton, which by then had become somewhat more civilized, but he never forgot his experience there and could hardly ever bring himself to visit them, though at home he loved their company and encouraged them to express their own views and to argue with him.

Family life at Hatfield in the 1870s when the children were growing up, was, indeed, very un-Victorian. Lord and Lady Salisbury allowed their five boys and two girls complete freedom to ride about the park, to clamber over the roof and to play games in the vast corridors of the old house. Their own high standard of morality, their devotion to each other and, above all, their sense of fun and their intelligence, set an example which the children followed quite naturally. As soon as they were old enough, they had meals in the dining-room and stayed up late in the evening, sharing family jokes and family pleasures and revelling in the heated discussions on politics and religion that stretched their young minds and made them think for themselves. Even when the house was full of distinguished guests, the children were allowed to mix freely with their elders and many an important visitor walking in the Long Gallery was startled to be suddenly confronted by an untidy 14-year-old boy, whose intelligent questions demanded a satisfactory answer. Uninhibited, lively and full of fun the Cecil boys and girls developed as individuals and 'their mode of life, with its mixture of privilege and freedom, animal energy and moral purpose, gave them extraordinary self-confidence.'

Lady Maud and Lady Gwendolin Cecil were educated at home, but the lack of restriction they as well as their brother enjoyed at Hatfield was most unusual. As a rule, boys in their teens, and especially elder sons, were given far more opportunity to acquire experience than girls of the same age. 'Cleverness' was frowned upon and any marked aptitude for study discouraged as unladylike, for work that exercised a girl's brain was thought to be detrimental to her health and damaging to her moral sensitivity. It was better that she should know too little than too much, perhaps because knowledge in women was subconsciously identified with the fall of Adam and Eve and an enquiring mind could well lead to temptation. Natural questions on sex were answered with elaborate euphemisms or dismissed with such prudish disfavour, they immediately became associated with a sense of wickedness and sin. For chastity and purity were deemed essential in young girls hoping to find a husband when they put their hair up and left the schoolroom, and innocence of the ways of the world their chief attraction. How much strain all this suppression of their adolescent feelings put upon them showed itself in their delicate health and the many ailments that disturbed their equilibrium. Yet they were often more resilient than they appeared to be and, in spite of the intense filial respect they had for their parents, not always so unadventurous as they seemed.

In big families like the Lytteltons and the Gladstones devotion to the Church was a strong emotional force that brought the young and the old together. Lucy Lyttelton, at the age of 12, was overwhelmed by her Confirmation. 'I know that I shall never forget the touch of the hand on my head,' she wrote in her diary, 'and the glorious rush of trembling calm that followed the indescribable feeling.... And then I went back and knelt down ... and the new life had begun.' Later, after her mother's death and her elder sister's marriage, when she was still only 19, she took on the management of her father's household at Hagley, instructing her younger brothers and sisters in the principles of her own abiding faith in the gospel of the High Church. And it was an argument with Lord Frederick Cavendish on a point of doctrine that first drew his attention to her when she was staying at Chatsworth in 1863. The second son of the Duke of Devonshire and brother to Harty-Tarty, he was so impressed by Lucy's sincerity and her charm, he went over to the Gladstones' home at Hawarden a fortnight later to see her again and it was quite obvious to everyone that his attentions were 'very marked'. Catherine Gladstone believed he was 'committed and decided', as indeed he was, but there was some anxiety about whether he really understood the true meaning of Tractarianism and these doubts had to be resolved before his proposal could be seriously considered and Lucy given to him in marriage.

She remained devoted to her own family in preference to her in-laws, whose style of living was so much richer and grander than anything she had known at Hagley. Being already related to the Devonshires through her grandmother there was no question of inequality of birth in the marriage, but after being surrounded by all her brothers and sisters and Gladstone cousins, Lucy found the Duke a formidable and taciturn character and Chatsworth somewhat oppressive. To her great regret she had no children of her own and her marriage came to a tragic end when Lord Frederick was assassinated in Dublin in 1882.

79 The children of the 4th Lord Lyttelton and his wife, Mary. (*Back row left to right*) Neville, Charles, May, Spencer, Albert. (*Second row*) Alfred (*seated*), Lucy, Arthur, Meriel (*seated*), Edward, Lavinia (*seated*), and Bob

Meanwhile her younger sisters, Lavinia and May, were old enough to emerge from the schoolroom for their first London season in 1868. Lucy generously paid for everything and looked after them and both girls were much admired. Lavinia was successfully wooed by Edward Talbot, a high-minded young man, who, at the age of 25 was offered the headship of the new Tractarian College at Oxford named after John Keble, where she settled quite happily and in due time gave birth to five children. May was not so fortunate. At 18, after being the ugly duckling of the family, she suddenly developed into the most beautiful of all the Lyttelton girls, with a mass of dark auburn hair, wide-set brown eyes and a radiance that was enchanting. She was also the most susceptible, falling in love with Edward Denison, a man 10 years older than herself with an idealistic outlook and an intellectual background. As the nephew of John Evelyn Denison, the Speaker of the House of Commons, and heir to his rich estate in Nottinghamshire, Edward was socially acceptable to the Lytteltons, but for some unknown reason his wealthy uncle refused to countenance the engagement and packed him off on a long sea voyage to Australia, where he died quite suddenly from consumption.

May's grief unsettled her febrile nature. Like her father she suffered from periods of black depression and nervous debility alternating with a wild gaiety, but unlike the rest of her family, she was rebellious and had a great appetite for admiration. After flirting — quite shamelessly, Lavinia thought — with several attractive young men, she fell in love again with an Oxford undergraduate, called Rutherford Graham. The Lytteltons disapproved. Rutherford Graham was the eldest son of a very rich self-made man in trade and a Presbyterian; and what was worse, he had a reputation for playing fast and loose with the young ladies of his acquaintance, besides being ambitious to get into the 10th Hussars, a regiment notorious for the immorality of its officers. May was forbidden to see him or to communicate with him and had to be content with watching this handsome, gay and amusing young man from a distance at a concert in St James's Hall.

Then fate stepped in — for Rutherford Graham, like Edward Denison, died suddenly at Liverpool on his way to America and poor May was left utterly distraught. In her diary she wrote of 'the dreary monotony in never caring to go to one place more than another' and of 'hating the sun and the horrid smirking people riding in the Row.' No one, it seemed, could help her. She felt isolated from her family, empty and haunted. Yet one of her brother's friends, Arthur Balfour, having at first pursued her cousin, Mary Gladstone, transferred his affections to her and hovered round her like a moth drawn towards a flame. Apparently too shy, or too irresolute, to propose, he left it too late. In 1875 May caught typhoid and, too weary of her young life to fight the disease, died on Palm Sunday at the age of 25. Arthur Balfour could not face going into the church for her funeral, he sat outside, weeping.

May Lyttelton was an accomplished pianist and so was Mary Gladstone, but any idea of putting their talents to professional purposes would have been vetoed at once; and there was little enough to occupy the minds of most girls brought up in the conventional world of the upper-class schoolroom, so that it was not surprising if they found their sudden entry into Society unsettling. They were expected to be entertaining and submissive at one and the same time, to be able to hold a running conversation with their neighbour at a dinner party without ever having seen him in their lives before and to attract the right partners at their first ball. If a girl became a wallflower, she suffered agonies of shame and humiliation and and was liable to be nagged by her mother. If, on the other hand, she was too oncoming and danced too often with the same partner, she put herself in the position of being 'talked about'. It was all *très difficile.* Hedged about with restrictions, admonitions and taboos, the Victorian young lady was skating on the thinnest of thin ice between what she should, or should not do, to obtain a husband. The miracle was that with so little intimacy permitted between the young of both sexes at this vital moment, she so often succeeded in adapting herself to the man she married and managed to live more or less happily with him for the rest of her life.

8
The Servants

The amenities of Victorian upper-class life depended on the numbers of servants employed indoors and out, and as there never seemed to be any lack of village boys and girls willing to go into domestic service, there was never any shortage of staff in the great country and town houses of the aristocracy. It was a hard life at the bottom of the scale in the kitchen, the pantry, the housemaids' room, the dairy, the stables or the garden, and the hierarchy of the Servants' Hall was even more rigid than the solemn ritual of the family upstairs. Servants were more snobbish than their masters and carefully graded according to their skills, the number of years they had been in service and their status in the household. Yet there was always the chance for a boy or a girl to rise to a more responsible post and compared with the frightful conditions of labour in the factories, life in one of the big country houses was much healthier and more rewarding. Youngsters might be chivied hither and thither by the butler or the housekeeper, but they had greater security than the industrial workers, who could be laid off through no fault of their own in bad times and left to starve in the foul back-to-back tenements they inhabited. Only if a servant seriously misbehaved was he or she dismissed and sent away in disgrace. The attitude of the nobility and gentry towards their servants was paternalistic and on the whole very generous.

At Belvoir, the Duke of Rutland employed a vast army indoors and out. On his birthday, with the servants of the guests who were staying at the Castle, no less than 145 of them sat down to dinner in the Servants' Hall, and when Charles Greville and some of the other visitors looked in on them, 'they had just done dinner and were drinking the Duke's health, singing and speechifying with vociferous applause.... I never knew,' he observed, 'that oratory had got down into the Servants' Hall, but learned that it is the custom for those to whom the gift of the gab has been vouchsafed to harangue the others, the palm of eloquence being given to Mr Tapps, the head coachman, a man of great abdominal dignity, whose Ciceronian brows are adorned with an ample flaxen wig.'

Mr Tapps, as one of the upper servants with a cohort of grooms and stable boys under him, was responsible for maintaining the superb coach-horses and the innumerable vehicles belonging to the Duke. His harness-room smelt of brass polish, matured leather and the juice of the tobacco he chewed, and was hung with bits and traces and horse collars polished to perfection. Having driven his Lordship for years, he was a past master at getting the best out of his horses and at keeping all the family carriages in mint condition. These ranged from the wonderfully ornate state coach with its armorial bearings framed in gold on the door panels, through a variety of smart town and country barouches of different designs and weights, to the shooting-breaks and omnibuses used to convey luggage and staff from one family residence to another.

This particular operation required a great deal of careful organisation on the part of the head coachman and even with the development of the railway network, was a highly complicated manoeuvre. Though her household was not on the scale of the ducal families, the Dowager Lady Sitwell, on her annual summer migration from Surrey to Yorkshire, made special arrangements with the Great Northern Railway, travelling in a saloon coach and another carriage from Shalford Station via Dorking, London Bridge and King's Cross to Scarborough, 'without changing'. How the Great Northern managed to convey her party 'without changing' from London Bridge to King's Cross remains a mystery. But her daughter, Florence, was up at 5.30 a.m. 'desperately busy to the last', and the party consisted of her mother and herself, 'our maids', Wilkinson the cook, two housemaids, Bessie and Florence, the butler and his wife, George the footman and Hill the coachman, plus four horses, a carriage and six Samoyed dogs. On arriving at Scarborough, everyone was extremely tired and 'quite done up', and it was the coachman's job to get the carriage off the railway truck and the horses harnessed to it to complete the journey. Fortunately Hill was a steady character, unlike Lady Sitwell's previous coachman, James Broadbent, whose fondness for the bottle had ended in his discharge from the duties he was often too drunk to perform.

By making such extensive arrangements in advance with the Great Northern Railway, Lady Sitwell succeeded in accomplishing her journey without getting herself and her servants mixed up with the other passengers travelling on the same train. Another aristocratic lady, the Countess of Zetland, with a similar desire to avoid the *hoi polloi,* had her own private chariot strapped to the rolling stock at Darlington, whence it was carried forward with the rest of the train to London. With her personal maid sitting beside her, all went well until soon after the train left Leicester, when the Countess thought she could smell something burning and ordered her maid to let down the window. Immediately a shower of red-hot sparks smothered them both and the Countess realized with horror that the rear of her chariot was on fire. Waving her handkerchief and shouting 'Fire!', she did her best to attract the attention of the 'policemen' or signalmen down the line, 'none of them', as she huffily reported afterwards, 'taking the slightest notice'. Meanwhile her poor maid, in spite of her mistress's plea to remain calm, became so panic-stricken she opened the door and climbed out of the carriage on to the truck and 'gathering her cloak about her', was swept away as the train rushed on. The

Countess herself clung desperately to the fore-part of her burning chariot until the train came to a halt at Rugby and her dreadful plight was discovered. An engine was sent back to look for her maid, who was found in 'almost a hopeless state' with a fractured skull and three fingers missing.

Rather unkindly, the Countess of Zetland pointed out that if her unfortunate maid had not been so foolish, she might have survived the ordeal in better shape. As it was she pitied herself for having to engage another woman, since a good lady's maid was hard to come by. It was necessary for her to be sober and discreet, 'refined in looks, voice and manner', always on call and never assertive. Moreover, great skill was required of her. She had to be expert in hairdressing, with a knowledge of how to use curling tongs heated on a little methylated stove and how to arrange the fashionable piled up coiffeurs with pads and false pieces, decorative combs and hair-pins. She had to look after her lady's extensive wardrobe – the underclothes of cambric and linen trimmed with lace and *broiderie Anglaise*; the corsets of whalebone with intricate front and back lacing; the shoes and stockings; the stiff gowns with their long skirts and tight bodices; the braided mantles and heavy furs; the muffs and tippets and accessories of all kinds: gloves, parasols, reticules, handkerchieves, floral posies of artificial flowers, feather fans and jewellery.

So much time all through the day was spent by a fashionable lady in dressing and undressing and her clothes were so elaborate, she was quite helpless without her maid, who needed nimble fingers for all the hooking and buttoning that went on before zip fasteners were invented. Lady Ida Sitwell had no idea how to lace up her own shoes and was not only quite incapable of doing so, but would have thought it very ill-bred and middle class to perform such a menial chore for herself. Her maid, Fowler, according to Osbert, was 'a prim, long-suffering woman'. She would 'edge' into his mother's bedroom, 'holding a newly arrived or newly brushed dress at arm's length, as though it were a corpse instead of an object of pride to her.' But she was an excellent maid and more than once had to stop Osbert as a child trying to eat his mother's hat-pins or otherwise causing chaos among the silver-backed hairbrushes, bottles and jars of scent and other trinkets on her dressing-table. Everything was tidied up and put back into place, for Fowler was never at a loss and knew exactly where to find anything and when to make herself scarce. She travelled everywhere with her mistress, packing and unpacking in layers of tissue paper the huge domed trunks and hatboxes needed to carry Lady Ida's personal belongings abroad to Italy or from Renishaw to Londesborough Lodge; and although travelling gave the poor woman a headache and made her feel sick, she never complained. Lady Ida's comfort came first.

A lady's maid, by the nature of her work, enjoyed a greater intimacy with her mistress than any other member of the staff and sometimes saw and heard more than it was good for her to know of what went on in her lady's boudoir or bedroom. As a go-between in any romantic adventure, her silence depended on how devoted she was, but few can have had such a nerve-wracking experience as Lady Florence Paget's maid when she accompanied her young mistress to Marshall & Snelgrove's one day in 1864. Lady Florence, the beautiful daughter of the Marquess of Anglesey, was engaged to Henry Chaplin and unbeknown to him in love with another man. On that particular morning she left her fiancé at the Oxford Street entrance to the fashionable store while she went to the lingerie department to see about her trousseau – and he was still waiting there long after she and her maid had hurried out of the shop by the door into Henrietta Street, where the Marquess of Hastings was waiting to carry her off with a special marriage license in the pocket of his coat. Her maid was a witness at the ceremony and loyal to her mistress, but the marriage was unhappy, which, it was thought, was a just reward for Lady Florence's outrageous behaviour.

80 Mary Webster, the housekeeper at Erddig. The housekeeper's room was the drawing-room of the upper servants. She held the keys to the store cupboards and ruled over the female staff

Loyalty and devotion to the lady of the house also inspired the long and faithful service of the women who acted as housekeepers. Their responsibilities were exacting and their wages – from £50 to £70 a year – were considered to be very high. But a good housekeeper had absolute authority over the female servants in the household and a status equivalent to the butler or the steward. Nothing could be done without her approval. She supervized every detail to do with cleaning the house and keeping the linen, the curtains, carpets and upholstery in good repair – a mammoth task in the big mansions with 30 or 40 bedrooms, long corridors and handsome reception rooms filled to overflowing with velvet and damask hangings, chintz chair covers, tapestry-seated soafas, linen blinds and embroidered bedspreads. She kept all the keys to the store cupboards, which were never opened without her permission, gave out medicines when they were needed and directed the housemaids, the still-room and laundry maids in their work, besides keeping accounts of every penny that was spent and dealing diplomatically with any problems that arose. The housekeeper's room was at the centre of the domestic quarters. It was her private parlour where the still-room maid brought her breakfast and her tea and waited on her, and also the drawing-room of the upper servants after dinner, where she entertained the butler and the visiting lady's maids to a glass of wine and a little gentle conversation. Nothing escaped her attention if she was capable and trustworthy and had the interests of her employers at heart, and no household could function without her.

The Duke of Wellington had a housekeeper at Stratfield Saye who rejoiced in the name of Mrs Apostles. She was devoted to him, but she almost burst into tears when he told her the Queen and Prince Albert were coming to visit him. He had, in fact, done everything he knew 'to avoid the subject with Her Majesty' and when she would not be put off, was very apprehensive about the whole affair. He agreed with Mrs Apostles when she said that 'however comfortable the house was as a gentleman's residence, it was much too small to accommodate the royal party with any proper convenience', but he told her 'what could not be avoided, must be endured' and together they set about making extensive preparations. As neither the Housekeeper's Room nor the Steward's Room was fit for the reception of such great ladies as

the Queen's dressers and all her other attendants, to say nothing of the innumerable servants belonging to the other invited guests, the Duke hastily turned the laundry into a dining-room and had bells hung from Her Majesty's apartments to the rooms occupied by her retinue. He thought Mrs Apostles was making 'the most of the difficulties', though in the end the royal visit went off very well and the Queen said she was pleased with her reception.

Housekeepers stayed for years with the same family, apparently taking in their stride a change of mistress, when, as at Hagley Hall, the 3rd Baron Lyttelton died and his widow had to move out and hand over the household to her son George and his wife Mary. Sarah Lyttelton, with her usual understanding, was afraid that Mary would have to endure a flood of reminisence from Mrs Ellis, the housekeeper. 'I suppose not a basin of gruel ever made for me and not a pot of almond paste for the girls is omitted from her anecdotes of the family,' she wrote. But Mrs Ellis was a treasure. She was 'always beautifully dressed in black silk with a lace collar coming out to her shoulders and a close white cap with a brown front of little flat curls'; and although she was very strict with the housemaids and would not allow them to wear flowers in their bonnets when they went out walking, she was admired and respected by the entire household. The Dowager Lady Lyttelton did suggest that her wages were rather high, but she believed that good wages all round for the servants meant 'smiling faces, fewer changes and a right to refuse all

81 The servants at Erddig in 1852. Group includes the coachman with his whip, the butler standing between the cook and the genteel looking lady's maid and the handsome young footman in livery

perquisites', and Mrs Ellis was so devoted to the family she stayed with them until her death in 1870.

The Lytteltons were particularly kind to their servants and so were the Yorkes of Erddig, a spacious family house at Clwyd in North Wales. Simon Yorke married his cousin, Victoria Cust, a god-daughter and Maid of Honour to Queen Victoria, and they lived comfortably at Erddig with a full compliment of servants in spite of not being unduly well off. One of their housekeepers, Harriet Rogers, was born on the Erddig estate to the head carpenter and his wife, and entered the household at the age of 12 as a nursery maid, before becoming nurse to Mrs Yorke's four children, then her personal maid for 12 years, her cook and finally her housekeeper, when Mrs Webster, the previous housekeeper, retired. Both women served the Yorkes

82 Harriet Rogers served the Yorkes from the age of 12 until she retired sixty years later. Starting as a nursery-maid, she was promoted to head nurse and then became lady's-maid to Mrs Yorke and finally cook-housekeeper

faithfully and kept the household affairs in good order, Mrs Webster not only taking care of her employers' purse, but to everyone's astonishment leaving a nest egg of £1300 in the bank when she died.

The housekeeper's room at Erddig was on the same corridor as the butler's pantry and there was a good deal of friendly coming and going between the two when George Dickinson was in charge. He was a good-natured person and treated the under servants kindly, which was by no means usual; for butlers were inclined to demand too much subservience from their inferiors and to bully them if they did not get it. The pantry was their sanctum and if any footman or boot boy had the temerity to barge in without knocking, he was told in no uncertain terms to mend his manners. But discipline behind the baize door of the servants' quarters was very necessary. Without it a formal dinner party of 30 or 40 people would have degenerated into a shambles. The butler was responsible for the appointments on the table — the silver and glass, the spotless napery, the finger bowls and the wine. He had to see that the livery of the footmen was impeccable and their white gloves without a stain. If one of them made a mistake, he was roasted afterwards, or if his breath smelt of beer, he was told to go away and eat cloves until he smelt better. Thus youngsters were whipped into shape as the butler himself had been, when, as a boy, he had learnt to wait on the gentry and to push his way up to the ultimate glory of the pantry.

83 The servants at Erddig in the 1880s. Group includes George Dickinson, the butler, Fred Otely, the young footman and the hall-boy, George

Henry Moat started as a footman in Sir George Sitwell's household and became his butler, valet and major domo. He was possibly the only person who ever really understood Sir George and knew how to deal effectively with his neurasthenia, and he did this by retaining his own individuality, his sense of humour and his earthy independence of character. When Sir George went 'dotty' about something — a new invention or an old medieval practice he had just discovered and wanted to revive — Henry simply nodded and kept his thoughts to himself. But once in a letter to Osbert, he wrote: 'Poor Sir George, he really is an hero for his bed. I have known him often being *tired* of laying in bed, get up to have a rest, and after he had rested, get back again into bed like a martyr.' Such disconcerting behaviour did not worry Henry at all. He put up with all his master's 'fads' and stood up to him without ever losing his dignity. 'I once told Sir George when he complained he was seeing things before his eyes that he eat too many eggs per day and gave him the number 5,' he wrote in another letter, adding jauntily: 'He fairly bit my head off!'

For Osbert, scared of his aloof father and spoilt by his capricious mother, Henry was a godsend. His pantry was an escape from the school-room and the still more oppressive atmosphere of the drawing-room, where the grown-ups never seemed to have enough time or patience to answer any questions. Henry never told him not to be inquisitive or failed to satisfy his curiosity. His instinctive wisdom, jovial laugh and huge capacity for singing hymns and sea shanties — he came from a long line of Whitby sailors, fishermen and whalers — had an endless fascination, and as Osbert wrote in later life: 'I learnt more, far more from talking to Henry in the pantry at Renishaw than from more academic sources.'

Renishaw was a big, rambling, old-fashioned house, still in the 1890s lit by oil lamps which were looked after by an old retainer called Stephen Pare who was almost blind. The servants were astir in the early morning long before the family had awakened, the housemaids opening the shutters in the downstairs rooms, cleaning the grates, dusting and polishing and creeping noiselessly along the corridors to enter the bedrooms with copper cans of steaming hot water. There was only one bathroom in the whole huge complex of dressing-rooms, closets, anti-rooms and bedrooms — Sir George thought it was sufficient. Yet he had a passion for tinkering with the house and as he disliked architects giving him advice, he was always concocting his own plans, which meant a continual coming and going of workmen who found his instructions bewildering and his volatile mind quite beyond their comprehension. In the garden his imagination really took flight, creating new vistas and walks down to the lake, terraces on the hillside for his antique vases and statuary, and splendid cascades falling into the water garden below. Both his agent and his head gardener followed his flights of fancy with trepidation; a new idea suddenly sprouting in the brilliant brain under his grey felt hat meant more workmen about the place and yet another upheaval just when it seemed everything had been put into good order.

Happily Sir George never marred his house and garden with any specifically Victorian 'improvements'. His mind was too set on the past and his taste too austere. The *folie de grandeur* of the opulent *nouveaux riches* was another matter and their attitude towards their servants more severe. They believed in firmly segregating them from the family and that, to perform efficiently, they should not be seen or heard about the house. At Bearwood in Berkshire, built in 1865 for John Walter the chief proprietor of *The Times*, the servants' quarters were quite as extensive as the enormous mansion itself with its bold, pseudo-Elizabethan front, pinnacled staircase tower and cumbersome grand entrance. There was a butler's corridor off the dining-room, with a servery, the pantry, a plate-room and the butler's bedroom; a huge kitchen with a scullery, a pastry room, a game larder, a pantry and the cook's closet; a men's corridor with a gun room, a footmen's room, a brushing room, a cleaning room and two w.c.s off it; and a housekeeper's corridor with the still-room, a store room and the women's work room leading out of it.

Prudery forbade the female servants mixing with the male. They each had their own back stairs into the upper part of the house and only a very rash housemaid would have risked using the men's corridor or the footmen's staircase. A similar restriction seems also to have been applied to the bachelor guests in the main part of the house, for they also had their own stairs 'by which single men can reach their own rooms without using the chief thoroughfare'. Whether the young ladies of the family liked that arrangement very much is a moot point. Mrs Walter had 13 children and her daughters were safely placed in another special corridor with the schoolroom and the governess's bedroom close at hand.

Such rigid separation of the servants from each other and from the family did not make for happiness below stairs and the increasing departmentalization of their work made matters worse. If the still-room maids, up to their elbows in bottling fruit or making jam, could not get a smile from a knife-boy or a footman, life was indeed dreary. They slept in dormitories at the top of the house and had little time off that was not strictly monitored; for whereas the old, more friendly ways of the great aristocratic households were free and easy, the plutocrats of the 1870s, uncertain of themselves in their new role as country gentlemen, insisted on too much discipline. When they tried a different and less spartan approach and had 'the presumption to make their servants as comfortable as themselves', they were, according to Augustus Hare, no more successful. 'I went to Worth Park – the ultra-luxurious house of the Montefiores,' he wrote, 'where the servants have their own billiard tables, ball-room, theatre and pianofortes, and are arrogant and presumptuous in proportion.'

The kitchen in a big house was a world of its own where everything was larger than life size: huge ovens for baking bread and cakes, outsize stewing pots and stock pots, enormous fish kettles and vegetable pans, great rolling pins and long-handled ladles that were fit for supping with the devil. With no labour-saving devices and no refrigeration, though ice-pits were dug under the cellars for storing blocks of ice in the summer, the work was hot and hard.

Poultry and game had to be plucked and disembowelled, fish gutted and cleaned, vegetables peeled, sliced or shelled and carcasses of meat deftly cut into joints. The chef had three or four apprentice cooks under him, each allotted a working space for making pastry, sauces, salads and sweets; for in most households, literally everything was home-made, from the biscuits for the family's early morning tea to the soufflés and all the other splendid dishes served at dinner and the snacks or plates of sandwiches the guests took to bed with them in case they felt peckish during the night. Main meals in a big house might have to be served in five different places within a short space of time — in the dining-room, the schoolroom, the nursery, the steward's room for the upper servants and the servants' hall for the lower servants — so it was not surprising if chefs were inclined to be hot-tempered and dictatorial. The kitchen boys and girls who spent their time scurrying to and fro at the chef's command, scrubbing and washing up and scouring pots and pans, had a tough time.

Female cooks in the smaller households were less formidable, though they also could be rough tongued and sharp with their kitchen maids. They had a softer side for the children of the family and would often let them taste the goodies being made in the kitchen for the grown-ups in the dining-room. They liked their ale or a drop of something stronger now and again and were stout, red-faced women with vigorous, muscular arms and tired feet, overburdened by their long, thick skirts trailing on the floor. One lady thought they

84 Footmen were chosen for their height and lordly appearance to show off the grandeur of the household, and were impeccably dressed in knee breeches and silk stockings. George du Maurier

should wear shorter skirts. 'We suggest this in the kindest possible manner,' she wrote, 'for we do not object to servants dressing as they please or following their fancies in fashion, at proper times and in proper places. We are sure cooks would study their own pockets and convenience, and obtain the good will and approbation of their mistresses by abolishing the use of senseless encumbrances in their kitchens.'

Large white aprons were part of the cook's equipment and these were washed on the premises, for every house of a reasonable size had its own laundry with a wash-house, a mangling room, a drying room and an ironing room. The laundry maids, who needed to be very sturdy to withstand the steam of the boiling coppers, were paid from £8 to £10 a year with free beer and tea, and were sometimes permitted to take their puddings upstairs to their own dormitory and eat it there. The still-room maids earned about the same wages. They never penetrated into the main part of the house and never saw their mistress at all unless she came to inspect their work with the housekeeper. They would then have to make a little curtsey to her before going on with what they were doing, their downcast eyes unable to get more than a glimpse of her fashionable gown as she swept past them in a rustle of silk.

Outdoor servants saw a good deal more of their masters, for the territorial grandees and their sons were great sportsmen. The boys were put astride a pony almost before they could walk and led around the paddock by the head groom before being taught in earnest how to ride and to behave at their first

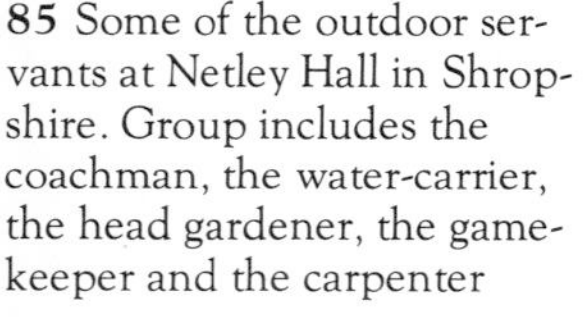

85 Some of the outdoor servants at Netley Hall in Shropshire. Group includes the coachman, the water-carrier, the head gardener, the gamekeeper and the carpenter

cub-hunting meet of the fox-hounds. They were encouraged to hang around the stables while the stable-boys worked at their endless task of grooming, feeding and cleaning the horses; and if they picked up some of the stable-boys' slang or learnt some of the things their parents were too shy or too prudish to tell them, it was all part of their education. Horses and hounds were of such importance to the aristocracy that often more indulgence was shown towards them than to the family itself, and if at any time it became necessary to cut down expenses, economies were made everywhere else rather than in the stables. The head groom and the huntsman were both figures of great significance, answerable to no one except their master and with a status in the countryside that compelled admiration from the local people.

Only the head gamekeeper equalled the huntsman and the head groom among the outdoor upper servants; but his job was more contentious, for the game laws were strict and unfairly loaded against the ordinary people of the countryside in favour of the rich landlord. This meant that the gamekeeper, as the custodian of his master's woods and coppices, was ever on the watch for trespassers and poachers, patrolling the ground like an arrogant policeman with a gun, at least until the middle of the century when the antiquated game laws were revised and the penalties for poaching reduced. Even so, shooting remained the sport of the rich and required a great deal of organization when the railways brought more guests than ever to stay in the country

86 The huntsman was responsible for his master's kennels and kept the hounds in top form, working all the year round for the fox-hunting season

houses and success was measured by the size of the day's bag. Pheasants and partridges were reared in great numbers by the gamekeeper and his assistants and the moors in Yorkshire and in Scotland were reserved for the annual massacre of grouse beginning on the 12th of August.

The gamekeeper had to train his dogs to pick up the birds without damaging their flesh, and to hire men from the surrounding villages to act as beaters to drive the birds towards the guns. And besides this he had to keep a sharp watch on the guests, who were not always as good at shooting as they pretended. One manual of advice to gamekeepers said: 'Do not forget the sandwich case and a flask of brandy to hand to the gentlemen, when their

87 Ned Humphries, the young gamekeeper at Erddig from 1866 until 1871. In spite of his open-air, healthy occupation he 'fell into a consumption' and died at the age of 24

88 *Opposite* Master Yorke out with the gamekeeper at Erddig The sons of the gentry learnt the lore of the countryside from the outdoor servants on the family estate

nerves get a little affected. Assist them in reloading, during which time let them stand as still as possible, till they get quite cool and collected. The trembling being quite off, proceed very deliberately.' Accidents did occur quite often. The Duke of Wellington at Wherstead 'peppered Lord Granville's face with nine shot', fortunately missing his eyes but giving him great pain, according to Lady Cowper, who dismissed the incident as 'unlucky'; and Lord Stanley of Alderley saw some 'wild shooting' at Glen Quoich, which injured his son-in-law, Lord Airlie.

What the gamekeepers thought of these accidents they never said. It was not the business of servants to express openly their views of the gentry who employed them. They knew their place and the best of them had what was called 'the happy knack of *never forgetting themselves* when they were talking to a gentleman.' But William Tayler, footman to a rich widow living in London, kept a private diary of his service, putting his thoughts on paper without reserve. It was a small household in Great Cumberland Place, Marylebone. Mrs Prinsep lived with her unmarried daughter and employed three maidservants — a cook, a housemaid and a lady's maid — besides William, who as the only man in the house undoubtedly felt a sense of superiority. The maidservants, he said, were 'very quiet good sorts of bodies and we live very comfortable together.' Mrs Prinsep did not interfere with him much — she let him get on with his job in his own time; and he slept and had his pantry — 'a comfortable room with a fire in it' — in the basement. Born and bred on a farm in Oxfordshire, he did complain a good deal of the dingy 'smoak' and the dark fogs of London, but he enjoyed going out with the carriage Mrs Prinsep hired from a nearby livery stable, except when Miss Prinsep kept him out longer than 'she should of done' and he boldly gave her 'a little row for it', which he hoped would do her good.

Another daughter, married to a rich banker, lived in Belgravia, where she often gave rather grand parties, 'hiring the best players and singers from the Opra house.' William thought they were grossly overpaid at 20, 30 or 50 guineas a time, as they were not there 'above three or four hours and most of them, of course, is foreigners or they would not be so incouraged.' He commented sourly that this was 'the way the gentry spend their money which ort to be given to the poor.' But at midnight when he went over to Belgravia with the carriage to fetch Mrs Prinsep and her daughter, being, as he said, 'one of the family', he had quite a gay time. First the footman gave him a tumbler of sherry, then the housekeeper invited him into her room and regaled him with sweetmeats and mulled port; and after sitting there for some time with the ladies' maids, he went back into the pantry, where the butler gave him a glass of champagne and another glass of sherry. 'I then began to get very talkative,' he wrote, 'and after helping wipe some of the glasses the butler gave me another glass of mulled port and by the way of finish he gave me a glass of sherry.' By then it seemed wiser for William to go up into the entrance hall to wait among the other less favoured servants until his ladies were ready to go home. Not surprisingly he had a bad headache the next morning and felt very poorly.

When Mrs Prinsep herself entertained, she hired two extra footmen to help William. On one occasion, after a dinner party with a menu of fish, soup, saddle of mutton, roast duck and green peas, gooseberry tart, orange jelly and dessert, some 50 or 60 people arrived later for a concert in the drawing-room. More drinks and refreshments were handed round — 'all kinds of sweet cakes and biscuits and different sorts of cream and fruit ices' — and a good deal of tasting of all these good things went on downstairs in the pantry. But William, who was writing at the very beginning of Queen Victoria's reign before Society had settled down into its more sober and refined era of fashion, took a very critical view of the guests. 'It's quite disgusting to a modest eye,' he declared, 'to see the way the young ladies dress to attract the notice of the gentlemen. They are nearly naked to the waist, only just a little

89 Upper-class young ladies, walking abroad, were escorted by a footman, who carried their library books and protected them from any undesirable encounter with the opposite sex

bit of dress hanging on the shoulders, and the breasts are quite exposed except a little bit comeing up to hide the nipples.'

He noticed plenty of 'false haire and teeth and paint' too, and went on to observe that 'sweet-hearting matches are often made up at these parties.... It's amusing to see the young ladies, how they manover to make the gentlemen take notice of them. They will loose their pocket handkerchieves or drop their gloves, that the gents mite offer to find them, or they will keep a wine glass or a cup and sauser in their hands until the servants is gone out of the room, so that some of the gents mite take it from them. The girls are up to hundreds of these manovers at parties to induce the men to begin talking to them.' Even so, he thought, 'there is very few that get husbands after all, except they are very handsome or got large fortunes.' But in spite of his disapproval of much that went on in the drawing-room, William had no regrets about being a servant. 'If a person wishes to see life,' he wrote, 'I would advise them to be a gentleman's servant. They will see high life and low life, above stairs as well as life below. They will see and know more than any other class of people in the world.'

9

Sport and Recreation

It was thought that 'the accursed revolution of railroads' would put an end to fox-hunting in England. Throughout the countryside in the 1840s, loud voices were raised in protest against 'the most oppressive monopoly ever to be inflicted on a free country and the growth of a monster which will rend the vitals of those by whom it is fostered.' The best hunting country, it was assumed, would be cut up into 'one vast gridiron', while the noise, the stench and the pollution of the railway engines would frighten the horses out of their wits and poison the air they breathed.

Lord Redesdale, Master of the Heythrop Hunt, resigned when he heard the railway was coming to the Heythrop country and became the arch enemy of all the railway bills that were promoted in Parliament. Lord Fitzwilliam fought the Great Northern Railway Company until they agreed to follow a different route that would not carve up the woods on his estate, which, he declared, 'from a hunting point of view are inseparable.' And behind all this agitation lay the fear that mechanical and industrial progress threatened to destroy the rural heart of England, where for centuries the aristocracy had enjoyed a unique way of life, dedicated to their sporting pleasures and the prosperity of their estates. If it was quick and easy to get to London by train, would the great landlords become absentees like the French nobility, an effete race lounging about in the city clubs instead of living fruitfully in the country? Or, if the *hoi polloi* of the towns invaded the country, how could the noble art of fox-hunting survive their ignorant behaviour?

In fact, the railways stimulated country life by 'bringing wealth and salubrity to everyone's door and the luxuries of the Metropolis to the Shires.' Hunt balls escalated into very grand affairs indeed and fox-hunting, though less exclusive than it had been, gained a new popularity. Lord George Bentinck could hunt in the morning in Hampshire with the Tedworth and get back to the House of Commons in time for the evening debate, his hunting pink concealed by a loose cloak or 'light coloured zephyr paletot'; and Henry Chaplin, Master of the Blankney Hunt and Member of Parliament for Lincoln, could indulge in the extravagance of hiring a special train which would draw up at a point on the track in Lincolnshire where his stud groom would be waiting with his horses to take him to the nearby meet.

At Badminton, the 8th Duke of Beaufort, described as 'a prince in his own neighbourhood', continued to spend a fortune on maintaining 'the most magnificent establishment of its kind that has been seen in our day', the lawn meet in front of the great house attracting 5000 spectators and the Duke entertaining 1000 visitors to the Hunt breakfast. At Belvoir, the 6th and 7th Dukes of Rutland with their famous huntsman, Frank Gillard, developed the kennels into a national institution. The hounds they bred there were noted for their even appearance and bright tan, their short legs and sturdy feet, and 'their blood was diffused in every fashionable pack in England.' Out of 200 puppies sent from Belvoir every year 'to walk' with the tenant farmers, only 36 were kept in the pack to achieve perfection.

But such a scale of private expenditure could not last for ever, and when the agricultural depression of the 1870s hit the landowners they were forced to take subscribers from outside, which meant a great change in the hunting-field. For whereas the aristocratic grandees and the country squires hunted because they liked it and because they had been brought up to it from childhood, the *nouveaux riches* took up fox-hunting because they were so desperately anxious to establish themselves as country gentlemen. It was a way in and a way up the social ladder. Anyone suitably dressed in a hunting coat, white doeskin breeches and black boots with brown tops, mounted on a fine hunter and subscribing liberally to the pack, could not actually be turned away from the field, unless he misbehaved by overriding the hounds or flagrantly disobeyed the Master. Possibly he could prove that he was not such a bad fellow after all, even if he had made his money in trade.

90 'The accursed revolution of railroads' was a threat to fox-hunting, but when hounds were in full cry, the engine driver was warned to stop and let them pass

91 Ladies entered the hunting field in the 1860s and their intrepid horsemanship more often than not startled the seasoned followers of hounds

There were also great benefits to be derived from the new order of things according to one observer, who declared: 'In sharing the sport of his superiors in rank, the young middle-class Englishman began to acquire the virtues and good qualities of a governing race, and to graft on his sturdy common sense ... and business capacity which have always distinguished his own class, the boldness, the dash and the endurance that are common characteristics of our aristocracy.' These were the men who went overseas to rule the Empire with the same spirit that urged them to jump every obstacle in their path in the hunting-field, the men who took their hounds out to India and hunted anything on four legs over the sweltering plains of Mysore. Fox-hunting gave them their education and the strength of character which enabled them 'to regenerate an ancient and glorious kingdom and to rule successfully an immense dependency of mixed races.'

Women were not conspicuous in the hunting-field at the beginning of Queen Victoria's reign. They were considered too delicate for the sustained exertion and the pace. Hounds ran faster than ever before, and the new fashion for gallopping at fences was very risky for anyone riding side-saddle, attired in the voluminous riding habits and plumed hats still *de rigeur* for the fair sex. 'Women generally ride like the devil,' Surtees remarked. 'They either "go" to beat the men or they don't "go" at all', and it spoilt the pleasure of the hunting men by making them feel awkward if they went ahead and left the ladies in the lurch. It was embarrassing, too, if the ladies fell off. How could a

respectable man assist a fallen woman in skirts on to her horse again? Or what might be revealed if her skirts were torn and her bodice came undone?

Nice women arrived at the meet in an open carriage to watch the proceedings, or if mounted on horseback, they trotted gently away instead of following the hounds. But in the 1860s, after her affair with Lord Hartington, Skittles settled in Leicestershire for the hunting season and joined the Quorn, whose Master was Lord Stamford, and though Lady Stamford objected to her presence in the field, her brilliant equestrian skill and superb figure in a skin-tight riding-habit worn with a plain black bowler hat, conquered all opposition. Shortly afterwards the Empress of Austria took Cottesbroke Park for a season with the Pytchley and from then on women were accepted. Lady Brooke hunted six days a week and Margot Tennant, 'unteachable and splendid', went out with the Grafton and the Beaufort, her bravado in the field shocking some people and earning her enormous admiration from others.

Not everyone in Society supported fox-hunting so eagerly, for in spite of the good example set by men like Thomas Assheton-Smith, Master of the Tedworth Hunt, who was out six days a week with his hounds but never failed to go to church on Sundays and was extremely abstemious in his tastes, in the minds of some people hunting was associated with heavy drinking and the dissolute world of racing. Henry Chaplin and many other rich hunting men owned race-horses as well as hunters and were highly respected in both worlds, but it could not be denied that the Turf encouraged gambling and, especially in the early years of Queen Victoria's reign, was a hotbed of corruption.

Indeed every kind of fraud, blackmail and deception was practised by the riff-raff of the racing world and some gentlemen of birth and breeding, who should have known better, did not act very honourably when their 'heavy plunging' landed them in debt. Jockeys, trainers and stable lads were bribed to nobble their horses or to spread false rumours about them to lengthen the odds, one trick being to paint the horse's nostrils with a concoction of starch, flour and water to simulate an attack of influenza when, in reality, the animal was perfectly fit and well. Dishonest bookmakers, horse dopers and informers crowded every race meeting, flouting the rules of the Jockey Club and defying the authority of the stewards, besides leading astray the idle young sons of the rich gentry, who fancied themselves as experts and were fair game for the touts and money-lenders. The hectic gambling connected with the prize-fights, cock-fighting and bear-baiting of the previous generation had been transferred to the racecourse, where the scum of the earth preyed on each other and their gullible victims.

By 1844 crime and deception reached a climax when it was discovered that the Derby winner, *Running Rein*, was a four-year-old horse that had been substituted by a series of dishonest manoeuvres for a three-year-old colt of a similar size and appearance. The exposure of the fraud was largely the work of Lord George Bentinck, who set out to cleanse the Augean stables of the racing world, partly to recover his own losses and partly to satisfy a lust for power in his chosen field of influence. He was a ruthless, arrogant, unlovable man, without the true integrity of his father, the 4th Duke of Portland; for according to his cousin, Charles Greville, who had quarrelled bitterly with him, there were 'serious blemishes in his character' which the world knew nothing about, and while he 'proclaimed himself as the stern and indignant vindicator of turf honour and integrity', in the past 'he had not scrupled to do things quite as bad as the worst of the misdeeds he so vigorously and unrelentingly attacked.' Lord George, none the less, did succeed in improving the standards of the racing world and when he dropped dead in 1848 he was acclaimed as a crusader whose fight against corruption had won him the title of Lord Paramount of the Turf.

Gambling could not be stopped by anyone, and vast sums of money were

92 Lord George Bentinck, who relentlessly attacked corruption and dishonesty in the racing world and became known as Lord Paramount of the Turf

won and lost on the racecourse. The 24-year-old Marquess of Hastings, who had stolen Lady Florence Paget from Henry Chaplin outside Marshall & Snelgrove's in 1864, lost £120,000 on the Derby of 1867, which ironically, was won by Chaplin's horse *Hermit*. Chaplin's victory, the Marquess said, 'had broken his heart' and he died soon afterwards, still believing that his own horse in the race had been doped. But Chaplin was far too honest to have done anything so reprehensible, even as a revenge for Lady Florence's desertion, and when he led in the winner at Epsom he achieved the highest ambition of every racehorse owner in the country.

The Derby was not only the most important event in the racing calendar, it was the greatest leveller in Victorian society, the one day in the year when all classes of people met on the same footing. An American clergyman on a visit to England, who got caught up in the crowd at Epsom by mistake, was astonished by what he saw. 'The first thing that struck me,' he wrote in a letter to his parishioners at home, 'was the mixed character of the multitude. Kindred tastes had brought together, upon this great arena, the extremes of society and in the closest contact. Here were the carriages of the nobility, emblazoned with their appropriate coat of arms and attended by liveried footmen, the cabs and carts in which not a few of the *ignobile vulgus* had been borne to the scene of dissipation. In the same throng, pressing forward

93 The Derby at Epsom: the most important event in the racing calendar and the greatest leveller in Victorian society

to gaze upon the exciting spectacle, were the gentry and the very off-scouring of the earth, clad in rags and squalidness. In the same group, or standing near each other, might have been seen high born ladies, servant girls, gypsies and the most worthless of the sex, all pressing forward in one broad extended ring to witness the races.'

The scene had not changed when Frith painted his great picture of Derby Day a few years later, but the Rector of St Andrew's, Philadelphia, naturally took a sterner view of the proceedings than the genial artist. 'How true it is,' he went on, 'that all the unregenerate, whatever may be their circumstances in life, possess kindred tastes, which frequently bring them together here and will assuredly place them in the same company and assign them to the same doom in the future world!' And after noticing the jugglers, rope-dancers, necromancers and gamesters around the course and 'the long lines of splendid booths and pavilions, which contained the appliances and paraphenalia of gambling and carousing on the most extended scale', the reverend gentleman concluded sorrowfully that 'it seemed as though there was here brought before me, in one concentrated and panoramic view, an exhibition of the world's varied allurements of sin.'

Possibly it was difficult for an American clergyman to realize the grip of the Derby on the English imagination as a day of carnival and gaiety. Yet there were sober and distinguished racehorse owners who disapproved quite as strongly of the gambling. Lord Falmouth was one and the Duke of Westminster another. His stud at Eaton Hall was famous and in 1886 his horse *Ormonde* won the triple crown of the Turf: the 2000 Guineas, the Derby and the St Leger. No one could accuse the Duke of frivolity — even Queen Victoria admired his high moral rectitude without reserve; but he was so proud of *Ormonde,* he gave a reception for the horse at Grosvenor House, and as it was led through the streets from Waterloo Station to Park Lane all the traffic was halted by the police to let it pass.

The Queen had some reason to be less happy about her son's racing activities. Surrounded by the Rothschilds and his other rich friends, the Prince of Wales spent a great deal of his time at the races and a great deal of money on his horses, gaining a popular reputation on the Turf. After his mother's retirement from Society, he made Royal Ascot the most fashionable race-meeting in the world, reinstating the royal drive down the course in a procession of open landaus attended by outriders in splendid scarlet coats and gold-laced top hats. And no one knew better than His Royal Highness how to please the waiting crowds on such occasions. Sartorially immaculate in his grey top hat and grey frock-coat, with lavender kid gloves and a diamond tie-pin, he set the tone of dignified opulence in the Royal Enclosure, where the *crème de la crème* of the social world gathered to give praise to themselves.

To most of the ladies the racing was a somewhat boring ritual of quite secondary importance to the fiercely competitive game of showing themselves off in the best and most expensive clothes they could, or could not, afford to buy. Something different had to be worn on each of the four

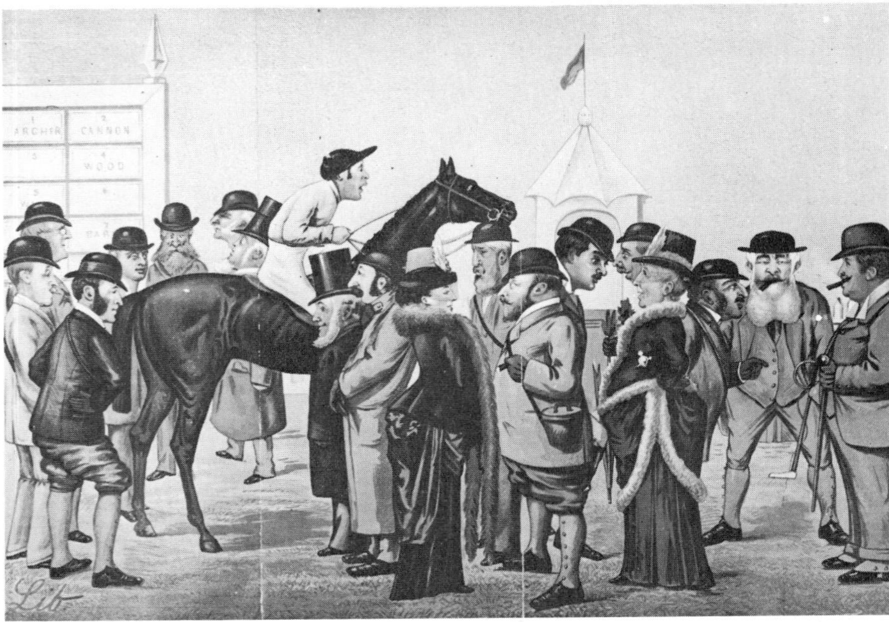

94 H.R.H. the Prince of Wales at Newmarket, talking to the Duchess of Manchester and surrounded by his rich friends. Group includes Lord Hastings, the Marquess of Hartington, the Earl of Rosebery, Leopold de Rothschild, Henry Chaplin and the Dowager Duchess of Montrose

95 H.R.H. the Prince of Wales reinstated the royal drive down the course at Ascot and made it the most fashionable race meeting in the world

days and this meant hours of energetic concentration beforehand with the milliner, the court dressmaker, the glover and the shoemaker and 'the purveyor of parasols, reticules and fans.' Great secrecy was observed among these people, and when the lady finally appeared *en grande tenue* she was satisfied if she could startle her husband and outshine her acquaintances. The weather was stoically ignored, though the wind and the rain often made hay of the most elaborate *toilette*. Long skirts trailing the wet grass of the Royal Enclosure were spattered with mud, tight bodices in the hot sunshine, on top of lobster mousse, strawberries and champagne, caused faintness or a flushed complexion, and hats as big as the Chelsea Flower Show, pinned on to swathes of thick hair, began to weigh on the head like a fireman's helmet. The Society lady needed all her courage and *savoir-faire* to survive a day at the races and to convince herself that Ascot was enjoyable.

Yet nothing had quite the same glamour or prestige. Ascot was the high point of the Season. All other sporting events paled beside the glory of being seen there and were more a question of personal taste or of filling up time from one social engagement to another. At Henley Regatta fashion decreed clothes of a less formal nature: flannel trousers, blazers and striped rowing caps or straw hats for the gentlemen, less elaborate day dresses or lace blouses

96 The royal house party for Ascot was a very formal gathering. The Prince and Princess of Wales are seen with the Duke and Duchess of York (later King George V and Queen Mary) and their other guests before setting out for the races

97 The Royal Enclosure at Ascot. To be seen here was vital to anyone belonging to the great world of high Society. Fashion ran riot in the 1890s when the ladies wore huge leg of mutton sleeves of lace and satin and hats trimmed with flowers and feathers. Arthur Hopkins

and long linen skirts for the ladies. Rowing was considered a manly occupation and was fostered by the universities of Oxford and Cambridge, the Boat Race becoming an established event in the spring. But at Henley the races were overshadowed by the social amusements, the balls on the house-boats covered in striped awnings and vivid with pots of geraniums and trailing vines, the delectable cold collations served in the luncheon tents on the lawns and the fireworks at night fizzing into the sky. For the débutante Henley was more fun than any other event in the Season. It was easier there to escape the watchful eye of the chaperone, to lie comfortably in a punt while some athletic and slim young man poled gracefully up the river into the shade of the willow trees, or to go upstream in a party of boats and step ashore somewhere with a picnic hamper full of salmon and lobster salads, stuffed quails and peaches and cream.

Any excuse was good enough for the elaborate picnics that fashionable Society so enjoyed in the summer time. The Eton and Harrow Match at Lord's Cricket Ground was another occasion when the top-hatted gentry were to be seen sitting on the grass guzzling platefuls of chicken in aspic served by obliging footmen. The public schools, like the universities, encour-aged manly sports and the team spirit, and again were a way in and a way up for the sons of the *nouveaux riches*, who mingled with the nobility and the gentry in the dormitories and on the playing fields. A boy whose father spoke with a north country accent could live his origins down if he were good enough to get into the first eleven and play for the school at Lord's. In 1871, some 600 coaches and carriages were closely packed around the ground as private grandstands for the lordly spectators and their families.

Middle-aged and elderly gentlemen, who had once been boys there, followed the game with great enthusiasm, and in the days of the great W. G. Grace cricket became a national institution, with moral overtones of fair play dear to the heart of every Englishman at home and abroad. Lord Lyttelton, himself passionately addicted to the game, paid more attention to his sons' prowess on the cricket pitch at Eton than to their studies. At home at Hagley, the boys practised outside the drawing-room window and on wet days in the long gallery, with apparently no thought of the pictures and the early Venetian mirrors hanging there. Only the Dowager Lady Lyttelton sometimes demurred. 'It is amazing,' she wrote at one time, 'how all our plans and arguments are mixed up with *cricket* nowadays — and all the time I understand no more of the subject than an owl.'

Women naturally were not expected to understand the ardent excitement of their sons and husbands for such masculine activities. Out of doors their movements were restricted by the clothes they wore and in the middle years

98 The Regatta at Henley. The floral decked houseboats were a charming background to an idle and pleasant afternoon on the river, the ladies shaded from the harmful rays of the sun by their parasols. Arthur Hopkins

99 Elaborate picnics appealed to the romantic spirit of the Victorian upper classes. Hampers of delectable cold food were unpacked and served with wine in the cool shade of the trees

of Queen Victoria's reign, even more by the prohibitions dictated by a moral and religious society concerned with their prime function in life as wives and mothers. It was indecorous and unladylike to run or even to walk at a brisk pace, besides being harmful to their health. Tight stays and thick underwear not only impeded progress, they caused fainting fits, headaches, heartburn and some of the more mysterious ailments common to the female sex. As a result, the ladies who were no longer in their first youth had few outdoor amusements and had to content themselves with presiding over the local or fashionable garden fêtes, handing out prizes for the best cauliflowers and turnips, or graciously presenting the village children with little bags of nuts.

Young ladies were a little more adventurous and in the 1860s became enthusiastic members of the Toxophilite Societies that sprang up all over the country, holding open-air meetings and tournaments, which became fashionable social events. Archery was a very attractive pastime. It encouraged poise and elegance and could be practised 'from childhood to green old age', for by altering the strength of the bow, it was adaptable to every age and every kind of physique. With a good aim and some style, young ladies could impress the spectators with their competitive prowess, and they wore special kid boots with cork soles to guard against any ill effects caused by standing on the damp grass. Emma Wedgwood, later the wife of Charles Darwin, and her sister, Fanny, were 'quite dragonesses' at their local tournaments, carrying off any number of prizes and afterwards enjoying the little heart-shaped cakes with icing on top in the refreshment tent, while the band of the local volunteers added to the gaiety of the occasion.

Francis Kilvert, the curate of Clyro in Radnorshire, was often invited to the archery parties given by the county gentry, sitting among the ladies under the trees 'while the arrows flashed past with a whistling rush and the glorious afternoon sunlight shone mellow upon the beeches in the peaceful afternoon.' 'Everyone about here is so pleasant and friendly that we meet almost like brothers and sisters,' he noted in his diary, and at Clifford Priory he found 'a crowd in the drawing-room eating enormous strawberries' and drinking iced claret cup. There was 'great fun on the lawn, 6 cross games of croquet and balls flying about in all directions' and all the girls were so pretty, the susceptible young curate lost his heart.

The sight of Daisy Thomas on the croquet lawn 'in a black velvet jacket and light dress, with a white feather in her hat and her bright golden hair tied up with a blue riband', moved him to ecstatic joy. She looked 'so bright and fresh and happy' and was 'so nice and sweet' when he talked to her alone in the garden, he went to her father, feeling 'frightfully nervous' and boldly announced 'I am attached to one of your daughters.' But as he only had one sovereign in the world at that moment and no prospect of advancement, Mr Thomas seemed 'a good deal taken aback' and Daisy was given 'a hint not to be too forthcoming.' Kilvert, tormented by love and remorse, was too sensitive to press his suit and too aware of his own impecunious position to have much hope of persuading Mr Thomas to change his mind. He kept the sprig of sweet scented verbena Daisy had given him in his pocket book and had to be content with worshipping her from a distance, though he felt very sad and 'it seemed as if the sun had gone out of the sky.'

Many flirtations begun on the croquet lawn had a happier ending, but before long the amiable game was out of date and a mania for lawn tennis swept like a wind of change through the quiet countryside, bringing the

100 Archery was an attractive recreation for young ladies. It encouraged poise and elegance and a competitive spirit

sexes together on the courts in a wave of exciting activity. The gentlemen wore knickerbockers and long black stockings; the ladies tied their skirts back with an apron which had pockets in it for spare tennis balls, and ran about with little straw hats pinned firmly to their hair, determined to show how athletic they had become.

'I am just learning and it is certainly livelier movement than I have indulged in for many a day,' Cara Jebb wrote from Cambridge to her sister in Philadelphia – and with the somewhat dictatorial tone she often adopted towards her nieces: 'The girls *ought* to play lawn tennis ... they couldn't have better exercise.' Besides it was 'a cheap way of seeing one's friends and much pleasanter than set dinner parties. I have a cake,' Cara added, 'a plate of thin bread and butter, and tea all set out on a table in Peterhouse Garden, and Kate in

101 Many flirtations began on the croquet lawn and this gentle game was played with great pleasure. Afterwards claret cup and little heart-shaped cakes were served to the guests in the garden

her pretty cap and apron to wait on everybody.' No one minded that Lady Jebb, while she was on the courts, wore a little black bag tied over her nose with a piece of elastic to keep the sun from damaging her complexion. She was already the queen of Cambridge society and only a very bold outsider would have dared to ridicule anything she chose to do.

The excitement of playing tennis in the summer was only equalled by the pleasure of skating in the winter, when the fens at Cambridge were frozen over and even the lakes and ponds in the milder areas of the West Country became solid platters of ice. Kilvert, returning to Wiltshire for Christmas in the very cold winter of 1870, went across the fields from his father's rectory at Langley Burrell to Draycot Park and found 'a distinguished company on the ice. Lady Dangan, Lord and Lady Royston and Lord George Paget all skating. Also Lord and Lady Sydney ... and Harriet Awdry, who skated beautifully and jumped over a half-sunken punt.' A quadrille band had been brought over from Malmesbury and as darkness fell everyone 'skated up and down with torches, ladies and gentlemen pairing off and skating arm in arm, each with a torch.' Chinese lanterns were hung all round the frozen lake and 'the intense glare of blue, green and crimson lights and magnesium riband made the whole place as light as day.' Kilvert 'had the honour of being knocked down by Lord Royston, who was coming round suddenly on the outside edge', and a 'sledge chair' was put on the ice to draw Lady Royston, Lady Dangan and some of the girls around. Harriet Awdrey, who was a bit of a

102 Lawn tennis became popular in the 1870s among the more athletic young ladies. They wore aprons with pockets in them for spare tennis balls and tied their long skirts back to give greater freedom of movement as they ran about the courts. George du Maurier

tomboy, hurled her half-burnt torch ashore while she was skating merrily and it hit Lord Cowley on the shins, which made him very angry, but she glided away with Kilvert's young brother to hide behind an island in the lake until his Lordship's temper was restored.

Such simple pleasures helped to pass the dark winter days in the country, where people had to make their own diversions far from the giddy excitements of the Metropolis. While the gentlemen were busy with hunting and shooting, the ladies, with too much leisure on their hands, had to occupy themselves indoors. They made albums of pressed flowers, gathered in the summer and dried off with botanical exactitude, or scrap books of coloured pictures of the Queen, General Gordon and Dr Livingstone exploring Africa, of pretty little girls in bonnets and in pinafores stroking their pet pussycats, and of religious scenes depicting Christ surrounded by angels with sparkling frosty wings. They did every conceivable kind of needlework – useful things for the poor and useless things for themselves and their relations: crewel work, Berlin wool work, embroidery, cross-stitch and crochet. They organized sewing bees in the village and taught in the Sunday school, and at home worked on the watercolour sketches they had made during the summer, sitting out of doors on little stools, with shady hats pulled well down over their faces to guard against the ill-effects of the sun.

A beautiful natural complexion was a great asset. Fashionable women had their face creams and lotions made up in expensive little jars by the leading perfumiers, but the not-so-fashionable country ladies went in for distilling rose water and crushing cucumbers to extract the juice which, it was believed, helped to enliven a dry skin. Make-up was only for 'fast women', those actresses Mr Gladstone abhorred as 'sinful creatures' waiting to ensnare the innocent and the unwordly. Yet in the 1840s Queen Victoria and Prince Albert had made the theatre respectable. They had successfully encouraged Mr and Mrs Charles Kean in their efforts to 'elevate' drama from the low state into which it had fallen. Without the blazing fire of his father's genius and without his tragic weakness for the brandy bottle, Charles Kean had become the Queen's favourite actor. He was such a gentleman and his wife, Ellen Tree, was such a lady – no whiff of scandal ever impaired their reputation; and it was quite within the bounds of propriety to invite them and their company to Windsor Castle to play *The Merchant of Venice*.

As the royal children grew up they were allowed to read plays and to act in them, and amateur theatricals became increasingly popular in the highest Society. In country houses everywhere, productions were staged with varying degrees of elaboration and were considered a harmless diversion for the family and the guests. The young people spent hours rehearsing their parts and 'getting up' the costumes, and if a masterful young lady could win more applause than a timid one and a jovial gentleman more laughter than an elegant young man, it was all great fun in spite of the tensions, the jealousies and the emotional strain.

Any thought of professional acting, of course, met with an immediate rebuke. There was simply no question of a well-bred young lady being allowed to go on the stage or to appear in public under any circumstances, either as an actress or a musician. Music, however, was a necessary accomplishment. Every young lady, talented or otherwise, learned to play the piano and sing, and though few of them had the advantages of Gladstone's daughter Mary, whose musical studies were encouraged by Sir Hubert Parry, they performed in the drawing-room to entertain the guests after dinner. A 'lovely touch' on the piano was a quality which was highly esteemed and a slight *tremolo* in the voice, whether from nervousness or faulty technique, was greatly admired. It gave 'the most affecting expression' to such songs as *The Lost Chord* by Arthur Sullivan, *In The Gloaming,* or *The Better Land,* the last of these ending *con tutta la forza* 'Far beyond the clouds, my Child, and far beyond the Tomb.'

Ballad writers of the period knew exactly the kind of sentimental song that would sweep the drawing-room singers and their audiences into an ecstasy of tearful delight. Amy Woodforde-Finden, an Indian officer's wife, set the *Indian Love Lyrics* of 'Laurence Hope', another officer's wife, to the most melting melodies, and her *Pale Hands I Loved Beside the Shalimar* was sung on every possible occasion. Tosti and Mendelssohn provided more ambitious amateur singers with charming numbers, and Liszt's *Hungarian Rhapsodies* challenged the young pianist to abandon herself to the spectacular rhythms of a virtuoso.

Queen Victoria's young Maids of Honour were required to play and sing in the evenings at Osborne and Balmoral, and though at first the Hon. Marie Adeane found it nerve-wracking to play piano duets with Princess Beatrice, she very soon succeeded in pleasing the ageing Queen and became one of her favourite companions. She was a very attractive, elegant young woman, tactful and discreet, and with a sense of humour that enabled her to survive the feuds and petty jealousies that so often simmered under the surface of the Royal Household. For life at Court was very restricted and rather gloomy, and the routine monotonous to a degree: breakfast at 9.30, luncheon at 2.00, a drive in the afternoon, dinner at 9.00 and a little music in the drawing-room before Her Majesty retired to bed.

Marie found the long drives in an open carriage on a cold day intolerable. 'We were not in till 8 o'clock,' she wrote to her mother from Balmoral, 'and the wind was so cold my face turned blue and then crimson and by dinner time I looked as if I had been drinking for a week.' Yet the Queen, so inconsiderate in some ways and so kind and sympathetic in others, inspired in the members of her Household a quite extraordinary devotion, and before long Marie's respect and admiration for her had deepened into a lasting affection. And there were diversions at Court from time to time, especially when Marie's bachelor uncle, the Hon. Alexander Yorke, was in attendance as Groom-in-Waiting. The Queen consented to be amused by his comic songs, imitations and cheerful anecdotes and enjoyed the amateur theatricals and *tableaux-vivants* he organized with great enthusiasm. In one of these representing *Carmen,* Prince Henry of Battenberg was a dashing toreador and Marie a dancing girl 'in very short petticoats'.

'The evenings here are quite cheery,' Marie wrote from Balmoral, 'and I am sure it does the Queen good to laugh.' She had always enjoyed Prince Albert's jokes, but there was little enough to amuse her now. She worked all day on her state papers and was frequently exhausted by the arrival of her ministers and the long discussions she had with them. And it was a very, very long time ago that old Creevey had noticed how 'she blushes and laughs every instant in so natural a way as to disarm anybody'. So long ago her plump round face had settled into a pattern of obstinate grief and she had almost forgotten what it felt like to be young and gay.

10
The Last Decade

The Jubilee celebrations of 1887 were a landmark for the ageing Queen. Fifty years of toil, anguish and glory had made Britain the most powerful and the most prosperous nation in the world with imperial authority over millions of people who had never seen the mother country. The Royal Navy patrolled the oceans, the British flag flew over vast tracts of land in Canada, India, Australia and Africa. British justice, fair trading and good government, administered for the most part by high-minded, honest and industrious civil servants trained at home to rule and arbitrate, had, it seemed, brought manifold blessings to the multi-coloured peoples in the far-flung Empire. In India the Viceroy sat upon a gorgeous throne, surrounded by a resplendent retinue of high-ranking officers, or entertained in the English rose-garden lovingly tended by his lady. Up country the lonely resident changed into a dinner jacket in the evening and with a bottle of gin at his elbow, re-read a five weeks' old copy of the *Illustrated London News,* while the untamed beasts of the jungle prowled about outside the compound and the native servants sat cross-legged on a mat outside the door. And nothing, it was thought, would ever shake this well-built edifice so proudly created by the loyal subjects of the Queen.

Pride in the peaceful progress of the nation at home also gave the English a feeling of superiority. Though agriculture had fallen into a decline, industry was roaring ahead and the labouring classes in the towns and cities were better off than ever before. The middle classes, working with diligence, temperance and faith in the Church or Chapel, had risen to a standard of comfort and respectability that satisfied their growing self-assurance, and the rich were very rich indeed. Only the poor remained: the 'deserving' poor, assisted by countless philanthropic schemes, and the 'undeserving', who, alas, failed to respond to any well-meaning idea of redemption.

The Queen herself had not failed in her duty. Even in the long years of sorrow and seclusion, she had worked indefatigably with her ministers: bullying, cajoling, sometimes losing her temper, sometimes winning them over with her charm, her palpable sincerity and the touching simplicity that had characterized her as a young girl. And when, after much hesitation, she consented to drive in state from Buckingham Palace to Westminster Abbey to offer thanks up to God for her 50 years on the throne, the people flocked into the streets to gaze in awe at the small, bonnetted head bowing this way and that to acknowledge their applause. Exotic Indian cavalry mounted on fiery horses, bewhiskered field marshals in plumed hats, kings and princes from abroad, Yeomen of the Guard and Scottish pipers, their kilts swirling as they marched, all added colour and excitement to the spectacle and emphasized the regal dignity of the dumpy little figure in black satin seated in her open carriage, who, none the less, in the midst of this great army and the shouting multitudes, was so alone, so ordinary and yet so absolutely unique. She was moved to tears – who would not have been? The once eager and active young girl, fond of dancing and singing, had become the revered mother of her people and the symbol of their greatness. Pride, exultation, affection and gratitude filled her heart and at the end of the long and tiring day, she said she was *very* happy.

Lord Salisbury was now her Prime Minister. Without the buccaneering panache of Palmerston, the enigmatic craftiness of Disraeli or the controversial reforming zeal of Gladstone, he had a steadiness of judgment and a wisdom the Queen valued very highly. She trusted him implicitly as a leading representative of all that was best in the aristocratic governing class and as a man of principle who had the courage to say what he thought without fear of the consequences. To the public he had the benign, aloof appearance of a mature father figure with an unruffled serenity and calm, which in some respects was misleading, for in spite of his patriarchal air of self-assurance, he was the least complacent of men with an ironic view of his fellow creatures. He had no use for muddle-headed believers in progress and was sceptical of too much interference in the lives of the people, whether from the Government or the do-gooders, his basic political aim being to preserve the delicate crust of civilization by maintaining peace and order through all the ferment of change he saw going on around him.

Deeply attached to his family, Lord Salisbury had always disliked fashionable Society. He was not a racing or a hunting man and he left the management of his estate at Hatfield to his capable wife. Intellectual argument, Greek philosophy, religion and the new wonders of science attracted him more than the visual arts, where he claimed to be a Philistine with no aesthetic feeling whatever. It was his duty as Prime Minister to attend the annual banquet of the Royal Academy and to reply to the toast of Her Majesty's ministers, but the private view of the Summer Exhibition, which drew all Society within the august portals of Burlington House on the following day, found him busy with the affairs of state at 10 Downing Street and as the century rolled on into its last decade, he was quite unaware of the infiltration into Society of the new Bohemianism in art.

Paradoxically, the Royal Academy, under the presidency of Sir Frederick Leighton, had never been more highly esteemed. Sir Frederick – the first artist ever to be elevated to the peerage when, just before his death in 1896, he was created Lord Leighton of Stretton – was a man of distinguished appearance, an Olympian god among his fellows, never stooping to an ignoble act and from the very beginning of his career *persona grata* with the best Society. He built himself a gorgeous palace in Holland Park Road, sparing no expense on the exotic interior decoration, which combined oriental and occidental art in a very striking manner. Visitors found themselves whisked out of the London gloom into the Thousand and One Nights' splendour of the Arabian Court, where precious stones, alabaster, marble and vivid blue tiles sparkled before their bewildered eyes and a fountain, hewn from a solid block of black marble, splashed and tinkled. Luxurious divans, tables inlaid with mother-of-pearl, fretted woodwork and engraved plaques of silver and gold, mosaic inscriptions and huge oriental jars all added to the Ali Baba magnificence of the room, described by one admirer as the most beautiful structure erected since the sixteenth century.

103 Robert Cecil, 3rd Marquess of Salisbury, Prime Minister and leader of the Tory Party in the last years of Queen Victoria's long reign: a patriarchal figure in the world of politics, representing the high principles of the aristocracy. Phil May

104 *Preceding pages* The annual banquet at the Royal Academy, the most august institution in the world of art, presided over by Lord Leighton who was *persona grata* with the best Society

105 'The Bath of Psyche' by Lord Frederick Leighton P.R.A. The academic, neo-classical school of painting was popular with the *nouveaux-riches* industrialists who had bought their way into Society

Upstairs in the artist's studio, the gorgeous east was left behind and the art of classical Greece and Rome predominated, with a reproduction of the Parthenon frieze at the south end of the lofty room, a number of plaster casts, amphorae and other antique props. Here Sir Frederick followed the meticulous method of work he had learnt as a young man, drawing each figure in the nude, then making detailed studies of drapery and applying them to tracings of the nude sketches, before transferring the whole composition to the canvas and working for a year or more on the painting itself. Patience and hard work brought success in the end and the high degree of finish so admired by his patrons. Psyche stood poised in an attitude of frozen gentleness before stepping into her Roman bath; Helios, the Sun God, having left his chariot in the sky, was seen on the margin of the sea embracing the daughter of Poseidon as she rose from the waves in the nude; and the three voluminously draped young ladies in the *Garden of the Hesperides* happily suggested an afternoon spent in voluptuous lassitude, perhaps as an alternative to Henley or the Eton and Harrow Match.

The classical myths depicted by Leighton, Alma-Tadema, Poynter and the other academicians of the same school all represented a golden world of escape from reality, from all that was contentious, disturbing and harsh in the daily life of the increasingly industrialized cities. The rich merchant princes, who had made their way up in the world, were willing to pay very high prices for several feet of canvas to furnish the walls of their large mansions and what could be better than a glowing, colourful picture of the Greeks or the Romans at play? Admittedly, the Bishop of Carlisle was shocked by Alma-Tadema's *Venus*. He thought that allowances could be made for the nude of an Old Master, but 'for a living artist to exhibit a life-size, life-like, almost photographic representation of a beautiful naked woman' seemed to him 'somewhat, if not very, mischievous.'

Yet in spite of the Bishop, the classical painters went from strength to strength. Alma-Tadema added bronze doors, a marble staircase and Corinthian columns to his house in St John's Wood and the Sunday afternoon private views he held in his studio were crowded with distinguished and wealthy people. Their carriages blocked the surrounding streets and the ladies wore their Ascot clothes. It seemed they could not have enough 'Art' to satisfy their appetite for culture. The same people went to the Summer Exhibition at the Royal Academy to see the 'problem' pictures, the paintings of rural and town life which told a pathetic or a moral story, and to see themselves hanging on the walls in commissioned portraits; for if photography as a form of art was beginning to develop, there was still nothing like the commissioned portrait as the grandest and most satisfactory way of perpetuating the dignity and prosperity of the sitter. Old, young and middle-aged gentlemen, standing very erect in dark, respectable clothing, glared into the space in front of them, while the ladies, with only their shoulders, their arms and their bejewelled necks emerging from rich swathes of satin, smiled icily down on the gaping spectators as if condescending to confer a benefit on them. Watts did wonders for the men, Millais for the women, and John

Singer Sargent, the American artist, painting the *nouveaux riches* with superb bravura, became the most expensive and the most successful portrait painter of the day.

It was, however, through another American artist that the Victorian world of culture received a shock from which it never really recovered. James McNeill Whistler had settled in London in the 1860s after spending some years in Paris among the avant garde artists and writers who frequented the Café Guerbois and whose clarion call, '*l'Art pour l'Art*', was soon to be translated on the English side of the Channel as 'Art for Art's Sake'. Even among the Bohemians of the Latin Quarter, 'le Whistler' was considered as '*un personage étrange, au chapeau bizarre*', because of the low-crowned straw hat with its very wide brim and dangling ribbon that he always wore. In London he appeared even more *outré* and though at first he flirted with the remnant of the Pre-Raphaelite Brotherhood in Chelsea, his talents and his Bohemianism were quite different from the stained-glass Gothic fervour of Dante Gabriel Rossetti and his disciples. The Pre-Raphaelites looked backwards in their romantic dreams to a medieval world of drooping maidens and chivalrous knights in armour; Whistler looked forward and found his inspiration in the magical mystery of the Thames, in the portraits he conceived as 'Symphonies' in black and white and in the Japanese prints, fans and screens he had bought in Paris.

His work was misunderstood and the rich patrons he hoped to acquire turned against him. But his enthusiasm for the Parisian craze of collecting blue and white porcelain quickly passed into the drawing-rooms of Kensington and Belgravia, bringing the gospel of aestheticism to the ladies of leisure who wished to be thought 'interesting'. The shop opened by Arthur Lazenby Liberty in Regent Street in 1875 catered for this new cult. Progressive ladies eagerly discarded the tight, fashionable garments of the court dressmakers in favour of loose, flowing gowns of hand-woven materials, the soft woollens of Kashmir, the filmy gauzes of India and the shimmering silks of China and Japan. They threw out the heavy repp curtains that weighed down and darkened their drawing-rooms, draping their windows instead in silks of different shades, hung in festoons and looped up in carved amber rings resembling Chinese dragons, and they bought latticework screens, blue and white ginger jars and tasselled, oriental cushions to scatter on the floor.

Punch made fun of the new Aesthetic Movement; Oscar Wilde, arriving in London in 1878 after his final year at Oxford, plunged into it as a means of drawing attention to his own arrogant personality. At Whistler's breakfast parties in Tite Street he created a furore, his vivid, epigrammatic style of conversation a match for his host's sparkling witticisms. It was not long since the painter's famous libel action against John Ruskin had publicly turned the great Victorian critic's conception of art as a moral force upside down. For Ruskin, who failed entirely to understand the avant garde artists, had gone too far when he accused Whistler of contemptuously 'flinging a pot of paint in the public's face' and the jury in the case had decided the words were defa-

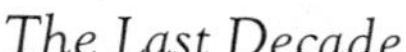

106 The gospel of Aestheticism preached by Whistler and Wilde, swept through the drawing-rooms of Belgravia and Kensington and it became fashionable for ladies to dress in loose garments and beads. F. Barnard

matory. Although the artist was awarded only a farthing in damages, as a result of his spirited self-defence at the trial, the doctrine of Art for Art's Sake was now at its zenith. Wilde adopted it with an exaggerated zeal and, much to Whistler's mortification, outdistanced him in dandyism and eccentricity. Soon it was Oscar not Whistler who was the talk of the town, and Bunthorne in Gilbert and Sullivan's *Patience,* who stole the limelight and set the fashion for the arty young man in a velvet suit and floppy tie at war with the Philistines.

Wilde, however, was not content with the aesthetic pose. After a successful lecture tour in America, he went to Paris and discovered in the decadent writers Baudelaire, Verlaine, Rimbaud and Huysmans, a *beauté maudite* that was infinitely more alluring, more voluptuous and more sinful, 'a pleasure that was poisonous, all shimmering in purple and gold.' Back in Victorian London, he cultivated a deliberately 'shocking', deliberately 'wicked' attitude towards everything and everyone, polishing his elegant Irish wit to a brilliance that enthralled his listeners. He moved from high Society at the parties of the rich and the elegant to the lowest society among the pimps and male prostitutes of Soho with unblushing bravado, undermining the accepted values of the conventional world and holding court at the Café Royal among his friends and his enemies.

Here, amid the Parisian style décor of gilt caryatids, marble-topped tables and red plush, came the artists and the writers riding high on the *fin de siècle* tide of ennui, extravagance and dissipation, and the upper-class voyeurs in search of pleasure. Ernest Dowson, 'desolate and sick of an old passion',

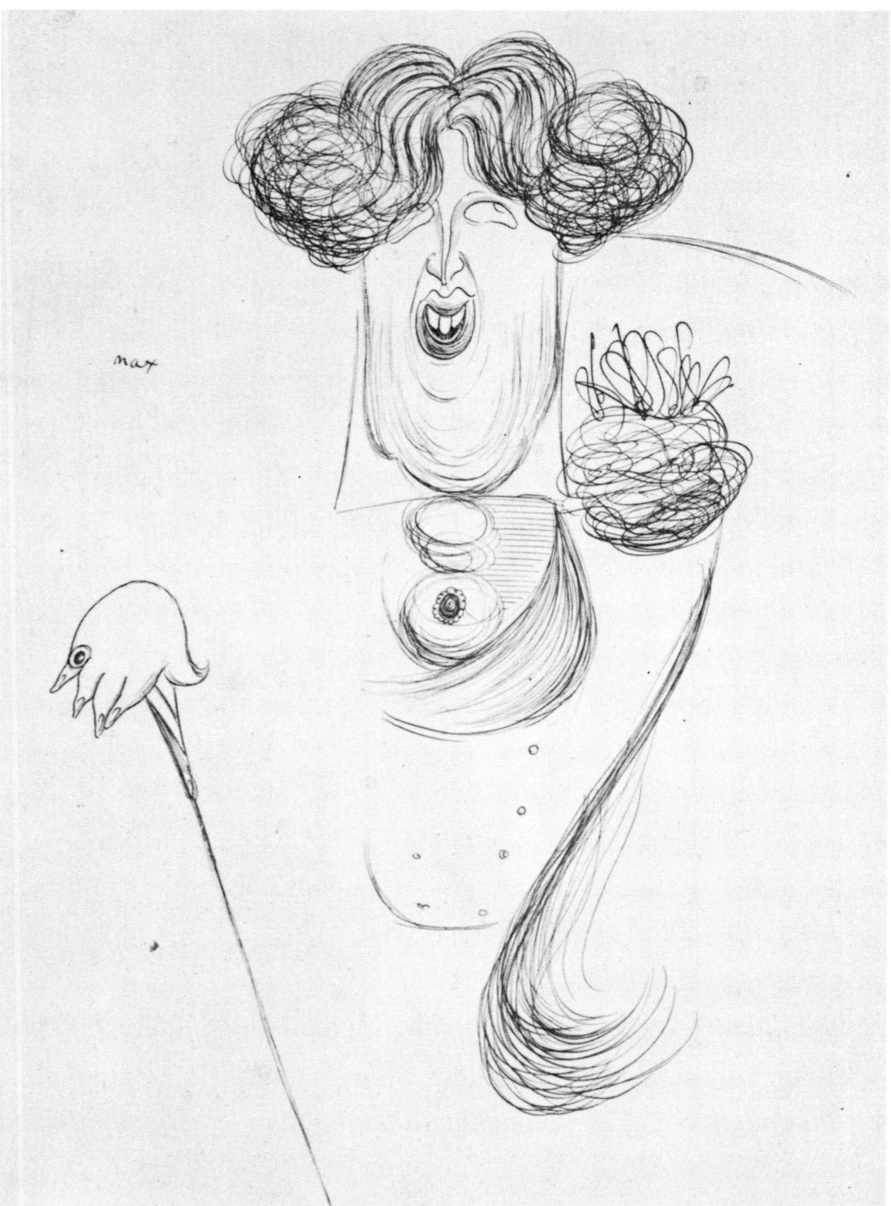

107 Max Beerbohm's caricature of Oscar Wilde, the brilliant Irish wit, playwright and raconteur, who dominated artistic Society in the nineties

crying for 'madder music, stronger wine'; George Moore, with his moon white face and fishy blue eyes, seeking a substitute for the stimulating café society of Paris; Aubrey Beardsley, feverishly working against time and tuberculosis at his brilliant drawings, which, in the depraved elegance of their line, revealed the secret inner world of his erotic imagination; and Max Beerbohm, a caricaturist of genius, fastidious, urbane and unruffled, a spectator on the fringe of the new Bohemianism, amused by its follies and aberrations.

London still had its leafy squares, its mansions on Park Lane and in Belgravia where the leaders of Society continued to give splendid balls and dull

108 Café Royal society in the nineties as seen by Max Beerbohm. The group includes George Moore, Oscar Wilde, Aubrey Beardsley and Max himself

dinner parties. But the gas lamps blazed in Piccadilly and Leicester Square, hansom cabs jingled in the streets, and the man about town, in his opera cloak and opera hat with his white gloves and his cane, was awake until the morning. The music halls were at the height of their glory and offered a marvellous concoction of winkles and champagne, toffs and swells, giddy girls and pint-sized cockney comics mocking all that was smug and conventional in the Victorian code of respectability. Dan Leno, Albert Chevalier, Vesta Tilly and the incomparable Marie Lloyd after her dizzy climb up the ladder from the Grecian Saloon in the City Road via Hoxton, Bermondsey and the

Old Mo', topped the bill at the Oxford, the Empire and the London Pavilion, appealing as much to the white-tied gentleman in the stalls as to the cloth-capped boys in the gallery.

No well-bred ladies were ever to be seen in the audience at a music hall — the entertainment was too vulgar. But at the Empire, the promenade behind the back of the royal circle, with its shaded lights and luxurious velvet couches, was a notorious rendezvous for the masher and the *demi-mondaine* dressed in the height of fashion with a bunch of parma violets tucked into her corsage. And in the theatre, the 'Gaiety Girls', chosen by George Edwardes for their statuesque and refined appearance, were hotly pursued by many a young Guards officer in defiance of his family's disapproval. Yet the frou-frou and the fun at the Empire and the Gaiety were a

109 The Empire Music Hall in Leicester Square. London at night blazed with gas-lights, hansom cabs jingled in the streets and the music halls were at the height of their glory

harmless deviation from the strict path of duty compared with what went on in the back streets off Piccadilly, Soho and Westminster, and particularly in the sordid house 'with heavy curtains' in Little College Street run by Alfred Taylor.

It was this house not far from Westminster Abbey that Oscar Wilde frequented, and it was Taylor's boys who gave evidence against him when he was tried at the Old Bailey and convicted of 'the sin without a name'. More damning than all his adoration of Lord Alfred Douglas, more demoralizing than the deliberate persecution of Lord Alfred's father, the Marquess of Queensbury, was the uncovering of Taylor's nest of unnatural vice. Society was horrified. All the snobbish and fashionable people who had crowded the St James's Theatre for the first night of *The Importance of Being Earnest*, melted away. George Alexander blotted out the name of the author on the playbills and when that did not disarm the indignation of the public, closed the play within a month. Oscar was ruined. The whole gaudy bubble of his fabulous reputation had been destroyed.

The Philistines were intoxicated with their victory. Nothing was too bad for the gutter press to print and nothing was left unsaid by the moralists in the pulpit. A sharp reaction against the decadence of the writers and the artists set in and *fin de siècle* became a term for the wickedness of a minority. None the less Society had been influenced by the Bohemian explosion of the 1890s and its mood was changing more rapidly than people realized. The rigid class structure that had given the nation much of its stability was beginning to crack as the middle classes and the *nouveaux riches* thrust their way into the aristocracy. Faith in the Church had been undermined by Charles Darwin's *Origin of Species* and a growing number of people calling themselves Agnostics claimed that nothing could be known, or was ever likely to be known of the existence of God or anything beyond material phenomena. Materialism, linked with progress in science and technology towards a bigger and better future, had, in fact, corrupted the minds of a new generation, and the moral force of the upper classes, where it still existed, was channelled into a new kind of aggressive patriotism, which reached its high point in the Diamond Jubilee of 1897.

This, even more than the Golden Jubilee of ten years earlier, was a display of Imperial might and magnificence, enviously observed by the Queen's eldest grandson, Kaiser Wilhelm, who had succeeded his father in 1888. 'In wave after wave of glittering ranks came the living evidence of the vast Empire,' one reporter wrote. 'Canadian Hussars and Mounties, giant Maoris from New Zealand, the Jamaican Artillery, the Royal Nigerian Constabulary, negroes from the West Indies, British Guiana and Sierra Leone, upstanding Sikhs, tiny little Malays, grinning Hussars from the Gold Coast and best of all, the turbanned and bearded Lancers of the Indian Empire, "terrible and beautiful to behold".'

Once again the spectators were moved to a frenzy of jubilation. Once again it seemed that Britain had surpassed all other nations in the world in power and prestige, for, as one writer declared, 'not since the Roman Empire had the ethics of one people governed so many territorial dominions overseas, bringing order and light into the the lives of their inhabitants.' And yet ... were things quite so good as they seemed? Some far-seeing members of the governing class were doubtful, if not downright pessimistic. While the elderly Queen continued to represent the Christian virtues of patience, charity and decorum, the middle-aged heir to the throne and the cosmopolitan Society he enjoyed showed every sign of becoming more irresponsible and more extravagant. Balls and dinner parties were grander, yachts bigger, racing stables more expensive and shooting parties on a scale that had never been thought of before. The new plutocracy was in the ascendant and the old aristocracy could barely compete.

Yet the greatest of all changes in Society had crept in without anyone being aware of its revolutionary possibilities. After years of submission, of being placed on a pedestal, protected, cossetted and overruled as the weaker sex, women had begun to revise their attitude towards the future. By the 1890s they no longer accepted a male oriented world where their husbands or their fathers knew what was best for them; they no longer saw themselves as bovine mothers of large families, year after year recovering from the strain of bearing one child after another or submitting to the ill health this labour caused. They wanted more freedom, more independence and a better education to prove that they had minds of their own. Idleness, 'accomplishments', domesticity and watering the plants in the conservatory were not enough—or not for the 'new woman' resolved to make a life of her own.

In the 1870s two ladies in Cambridge, Miss Emily Davies and Miss Anne Jemima Clough, and two ladies in Oxford, Miss Madeleine Shaw Lefevre

110 H.R.H. the Prince of Wales drives out from the gates of Marlborough House. The middle-aged heir to the throne was the undisputed leader of smart, cosmopolitan Society

and Miss Elizabeth Wordsworth, daughter of a bishop and great niece of the poet, established the first colleges for female students, named Girton, Newnham, Somerville and Lady Margaret Hall. Masculine opposition to the whole idea of women thinking for themselves was implacable in some quarters and the prospect of them competing for academic honours an anathema. Dr Liddon of Christ Church believed it was 'an educational development which runs counter to the wisdom and experience of all the centuries of Christendom' and Ruskin refused 'to let the bonnets in' to his lectures. But Miss Madeleine Shaw Lefevre, the first Principal of Somerville College, had an impeccable upper-class background and her students behaved with the utmost decorum. They dressed demurely in trailing velveteen gowns with wide lace collars and amber beads, and they did not, as some of their masculine opponents hoped they would, collapse in fainting fits at their lectures or attempt to flirt with their tutors. They gave modest tea-parties in their bleak, uncomfortable rooms and rejoiced in their freedom from the aimless existence of an unmarried daughter at home.

It was not only the studious young ladies at Oxford and Cambridge who were breaking away from the restrictions of Victorian home life, with its mundane domestic tasks and its countless prohibitions. Women everywhere were becoming more athletic, less timid, more ambitious. They took up golf as well as tennis, wearing skirts that were called 'short' because they came to the ankles; and buttoned up to the neck in one of Mr Burberry's raincoats, they were no longer afraid of getting wet, for, as he said in one of his advertisements, the special gaberdine cloth he had patented 'kept the body in a wholesome and eupeptic condition in all temperatures and weathers.' The ugly trousered garment Mrs Amelia Bloomer had endeavoured to popularize in the 1850s had never caught on – perhaps because Mrs Bloomer was middle class and an American; but Balmoral boots worn by the Queen herself, serge skirts and silk blouses, and sensible hats of tweed and felt became popular for sports and mountain climbing, and a few very daring ladies, wrapped up in veils and dust coats and and wearing enormous goggles, took to the new sport of motoring.

It seemed unlikely that any of them could be trusted to hold the steering-wheel of these fractious and noisy new horseless carriages, which, of course, only the rich could afford. But Mrs Bernard Weguelin of Coombe End, near Malden in Surrey, a lady of much grace and charm, acquired a 3½hp De Dion in 1897 and after an hour or so driving in the country lanes round Coombe Hill, 'to get the hang of the thing', drove herself all the way back to her town house in Pont Street 20 miles off without any mishap and without showing any sign of fatigue. Later she bought a 12hp Panhard and was often to be seen at the wheel 'negotiating down Bond Street and Piccadilly, to the utter mystification of all lookers-on, to whom the spectacle of a lady on a car was altogether new.'

If the appearance of Mrs Weguelin 'on a car' caused 'mystification', the sight of a lady astride a bicycle, when the fashionable craze for cycling came in, had a far more disturbing effect on the exquisite sensibilities of Max

111 Piccadilly in the nineties. Hansom cabs and elegant carriages rolled along the street, sandwich-men carrying advertisements walked in the gutter and well-dressed pedestrians strolled on the pavement

Beerbohm. 'Fashion,' he said, 'in pursuit of her other foibles, had always managed to look nice. On the archery-lawn, gazing so seriously at "the gold", as she drew back her bow-string, paused, and let fly her arrow; rinking, with her hands in a big muff and her fur cap tilted on the steep incline of her *chevelure*; at croquet, daintily imposing a Balmoral-booted foot on the ball ...; or as she wheeled hither and thither over the tennis-court – in such attitudes as these she was always a thing of gracious and delicate appeal.' Perched on a bicycle 'to pedal the treadles, she was an effort, an anomaly, a fright.'

The *Queen Magazine* also criticized 'the wheel-women of today and tomorrow' in one of its leading editorials. 'They are sharp, wide-awake, aggressive, self-assertive. They know no fear and what sense of shame they have wears a different aspect from their ancestors'. They stand no nonsense and need no help, save in matters pertaining to their machines.' But it was useless for the *Queen* or anyone else to cry out against the 'new woman' of the 1890s. She really did not care what the world thought of her, she was too intent on enjoying her independence, and if her mother and her grandmother thought she was making herself 'cheap', many of the young men in Society were captivated by her courage and her daring.

Margot Tennant knew no fear in the hunting-field and was equally courageous in flouting the accepted idea of how a young woman should, or should not, behave in company. With her sister, Laura, she took to enter-

112 Mrs Weguelin 'on' her car. In the nineties, a few intrepid ladies took to the new sport of motoring driving with dash and skill

taining her friends upstairs after her father and mother had retired to bed at 11 p.m. 'We wore charming dressing-jackets,' she wrote, 'and sat up in bed with coloured cushions behind our backs, while the brothers and friends sat on the floor.... The gas was turned low, a brilliant fire made up and either a guest or one of us would read by the light of a single candle, tell ghost-stories or discuss current affairs, politics, people and books.'

That these innocent, midnight meetings when they were discovered, should shock anyone, appeared 'fantastic' to this spirited, brilliant and utterly candid young woman, whose eager appetite for life was insatiable. 'With faultless nerve and thrust and inexhaustible energy', she blithely went her own way, telling people the truth, puncturing their pomposity and creating a furore of excited speculation about what she would do or say next.

113 The 'new woman'. Margot Tennant, who became the wife of H. H. Asquith: seen here dressed as an oriental snake charmer for the Fancy Dress Ball at Devonshire House in 1897

'Her wit and the wielding of it' made her the centre of a group of the most intelligent young people in Society called 'the Souls', but when it became obvious that Herbert Asquith, a widower with five children, was attracted to her, both her friends and her enemies were gravely disturbed.

H. H. Asquith was quiet and sober and at the age of 38 had a great future in front of him as the most likely leader of the Liberal Party. Margot was restless, irresponsible and the last woman in the world it seemed to sacrifice her freedom for the cares of marriage to a man with five young children, who disliked hunting and had never enjoyed larking about in Society. But H.H. knew what he wanted. To him she was 'a baffling, elusive little figure, sometimes tormenting, sometimes mocking, sometimes full of sweet gravity and a kind of wistful, almost compassionate tenderness, but always ... the light and hope of life.' She haunted him day and night. 'I am not going to overshadow your life,' he wrote. 'You shall have the overruling voice. But until you speak it, you are mine — to love, to live for, to worship, to enthrone, with a loyalty that nothing can shake.' And so it was to be, from the day they were married in May 1894 until the end.

'We kept together in an inseparable clasp of confidence and love,' Margot wrote of a marriage that never faltered through all the shattering experiences of a new century and a new world. For when at last the indomitable old Queen sickened and died at Osborne in 1901 and the Victorian Era came to an end, the heyday of Society had only a few more years to run before the lamps went out all over Europe and a new, more democratic age struggled to emerge from the darkness of the First World War. It gazed back without nostalgia to the cluttered rooms, the potted plants and the prim fashions of the nineteenth century, to the gentlemen in their sombre black suits, the ladies burdened with frills and petticoats and layers of silk and satin heavily trimmed with bugles and beads, the little boys in their thick Norfolk jackets and the little girls in their beribboned bonnets and button boots. How smug and complacent they looked! How desperately covered up! How stuffy and pompous and self-satisfied! How absurd! The reaction of the 1920s was violent — everything was pooh-poohed, debunked and thrown on the rubbish heap; and for a long time it was quite forgotten that behind the conventional padding, the hypocrisy, the idealism and the virtue of the nineteenth century, the Victorians, like ourselves or any other generation of mankind, were men and women with human feelings and human aspirations, adapting themselves to a changing world and attempting in the process to learn the unpredictable art of living.

BIBLIOGRAPHY

Askwith, Betty, *The Lytteltons: A Family Chronicle of the 19th Century*, Chatto & Windus, 1975

Asquith, Margot, *Autobiography*, Thornton Butterworth, 1920

Battiscombe, Georgina, *Mrs Gladstone: Portrait of a Marriage*, Constable, 1956

Beerbohm, Max, *Works and More*, John Lane, 1930

Blake, Robert, *Disraeli*, Eyre & Spottiswoode, 1966

Blyth, Henry, *Skittles: The Last Victorian Courtesan*, Hart-Davis, 1970

Bott, Alan and Clephane, Irene, *Our Mothers*, Gollancz, 1932

Carlyle, Jane Welsh, *I Too Am Here: Selections from Her Letters*, Ed. Alan and Mary Mcqueen Simpson, Cambridge University Press, 1977

Carr, Raymond, *English Fox Hunting: A History*, Weidenfeld & Nicolson, 1976

Cecil, Lord David, *The Cecils of Hatfield House*, Constable, 1973

———, *Max: A Biography*, Constable, 1964

Churchill, Lady Randolph, *Reminiscences*, Edward Arnold, 1908

Churchill, Winston S., *My Early Life*, Odhams, 1958

Cook, Olive, *The English Country House: An Art and a Way of Life*, Thames & Hudson, 1974

Cowles, Virginia, *The Rothschilds: A Family of Fortune*, Weidenfeld & Nicolson, 1973

Duff, David, *Albert and Victoria*, Muller, 1972

Evans, Hilary and Mary, *The Party That Lasted 100 Days: The Late Victorian Season*, Macdonald & Jane's, 1976

Evans, Dr Joan, *The Victorians*, Cambridge University Press, 1966

Fielding, Daphne, *The Duchess of Jermyn Street*, Eyre & Spottiswoode, 1964

Gathorne-Hardy, Jonathan, *The Rise and Fall of the British Nanny*, Hodder & Stoughton, 1972

Gaunt, William, *Victorian Olympus*, Jonathan Cape, 1975

———, *The Aesthetic Adventure*, Jonathan Cape, 1975

Gibbs-Smith, Charles H., *The Fashionable Lady in the 19th Century*, H.M.S.O., 1960

Girouard, Mark, *The Victorian Country House*, Clarendon Press, 1977

Greville, Charles, *Memoirs 1821-1862*, Ed. Roger Fulford, Batsford, 1963

Hibbert, Christopher, *Edward VII: A Portrait*, Alan Lane, 1976

Hill, Brian, *Julia Margaret Cameron: A Victorian Family Portrait*, Owen, 1973

Huxley, Gervas, *Victorian Duke: Life of the 1st Duke of Westminster*, Oxford University Press, 1967

Jackson, Holbrook, *The Eighteen Nineties*, Pelican Books, 1939

Jebb, Lady, *With Dearest Love to All: The Life and Letters of Lady Jebb*, Ed. Mary Reed Bobbitt, Faber & Faber, 1960

Kilvert, Francis, *Diary, 1870-1879: A Selection*, Ed. William Plomer, Jonathan Cape, 1944

Lang, Theo, *My Darling Daisy*, Michael Joseph, 1966
Laver, James, *Victorian Vista*, Hulton Press, 1954
Mallet, Marie, *Life with Queen Victoria: The Letters of Marie Mallet*, Ed. Victor Mallet, John Murray, 1968
Mitford, Nancy, *The Stanleys of Alderley: Their Letters, 1851-1865*, Hamish Hamilton, 1968
Nevill, Lady Dorothy, *Leaves from the Notebooks of Lady Dorothy Nevill*, Ed. Ralph Nevill, Macmillan, 1907
Pope-Hennessey, James, *Monckton Milnes: The Years of Promise*, Constable, 1949
Pound, Reginald, *Albert: A Biography of the Prince Consort*, Michael Joseph, 1973
Quennell, Peter, *Victorian Panorama*, Batsford, 1937
Ray, Gordon, *Thackeray: The Age of Wisdom, 1847-63*, Oxford University Press, 1958
Ridley, Jasper, *Lord Palmerston*, Constable, 1970
Rowse, A.L., *The Later Churchills*, Macmillan, 1958
Seth-Smith, Michael, *A History of Flat Racing*, New English Library, 1978
Sitwell, Osbert, *Left Hand, Right Hand*, Macmillan, 1945
– – –, *The Scarlet Tree*, Macmillan, 1946
Strachey, Lytton, *Eminent Victorians*, Penguin Books, 1948
– – –, *Queen Victoria*, Chatto & Windus, 1921
Tayler, William, *Diary of a Footman*, Ed. Dorothy Wise, Marylebone Society Publication, 1962
Trevelyan, G.M., *Illustrated English Social History, Vol. 4*, Pelican Books, 1964
Victoria, Queen, *Dearest Child: Letters between Queen Victoria and the Princess Royal, 1858-1861*, Ed. Roger Fulford, Evans, 1964
Warwick, Frances, Countess of, *Life's Ebb and Flow*, Hutchinson, 1929
Woodham-Smith, Cecil, *Florence Nightingale*, Constable, 1950
– – –, *Queen Victoria: Her Life and Times*, Hamish Hamilton, 1972

INDEX